5.5.

THE
OLIVE AND THE SWORD

By the same Author

MYTH AND MIRACLE
THE WHEEL OF FIRE
THE IMPERIAL THEME
THE SHAKESPEARIAN TEMPEST
THE CHRISTIAN RENAISSANCE
PRINCIPLES OF SHAKESPEARIAN
    PRODUCTION
ATLANTIC CROSSING
THE BURNING ORACLE
THE STARLIT DOME
CHARIOT OF WRATH

The Olive and The Sword

A STUDY OF ENGLAND'S SHAKESPEARE

By G. WILSON KNIGHT

> Bring me into your city
> And I will use the olive with my sword;
> Make war breed peace; make peace stint war; make each
> Prescribe to other as each other's leech.
> TIMON OF ATHENS, V. iv. 81.

> The mortal moon hath her eclipse endur'd,
> And the sad augurs mock their own presage;
> Incertainties now crown themselves assur'd,
> And peace proclaims olives of endless age.
> SONNET CVII.

Oxford University Press
LONDON NEW YORK TORONTO

OXFORD UNIVERSITY PRESS
AMEN HOUSE, LONDON, E.C.4
Edinburgh   Glasgow   Bombay
Calcutta   Madras   Melbourne
New   York   Toronto   Capetown
HUMPHREY MILFORD
PUBLISHER TO THE
UNIVERSITY

Published May 1944
Reprinted September 1944

PRINTED IN GREAT BRITAIN

PREFACE

THE following pages present a revision of a script composed in the early summer of 1940; though the section on *Henry VI* is new.

Their central argument has been variously presented in lecture-recitals and broadcasts and, under the title *This Sceptred Isle*, both in pamphlet form and at the Westminster Theatre, London (1941). Many presentations have since been given by the St. Cross Players. Such attempts have, necessarily, remained sketchy: at the Westminster Theatre I could do little more than concentrate on the three main pillars of Shakespeare's positive statement, *Henry V*, *Timon of Athens* and *Henry VIII*, with short glimpses of the negative in *Richard III* and *Macbeth*. But the time seems now ripe for the more detailed exposition.

I record my thanks to Mr. C. L. Brook of Stowe, for valuable assistance in the preparation of my text and the checking of references. Line-references follow the Oxford edition.

G. W. K.

Stowe, 1943

P.S.—I find that Prof. J. Dover Wilson's recent *Fortunes of Falstaff* makes contact with my thesis and have added a footnote (on p. 46) to point the relevance.

CONTENTS

I

OUR ENGLISH HERITAGE

FOUR years ago the sudden fusion of parties into a single united British front gave confidence and purpose to a nation in peril. Only when all parties are felt as, in the depths, at one, can the soul of a nation be revealed; as in a human life, when different attributes, body, heart, and mind, pulse together, the soul is known. So sudden a birth is perhaps a trifle embarrassing. A new thing has been hatched and blinks somewhat dazedly at the world around; and the soul of England has yet to find, or rather hear, its own voice.

We are still seriously hampered by old inertias and many indecisions. For what are we fighting? No doubt, to shield ourselves, and therefore many other peoples, from German domination : that is, we fight a negative and defensive war to preserve from worse evils a society which our own most incisive thinkers have continually condemned. We can, of course, point to our Christian tradition; but to what lukewarm conventionality, half-belief, and impotence had that tradition fallen! 'Tradition' is, by the way, too vague a word to provide a proper test. Dare we say, for example, that we are fighting for Christ? To-day a positive and personal imitation of—I do not say allegiance to—Christ will lead, as often as not, to some theory of pacifism; and though such pacifism must prove unsound while its holder supports a civil order based on ultimate force, for the difference is superficial only, a difficulty remains. Nor should we lay too great an emphasis on abstract concepts of 'justice' and 'law' (those self-righteous catchwords at which our continental critics scoff) without recognising that, though 'right' and 'wrong' may be ultimate, resting between man and God, 'justice' and 'law' exist properly only in terms of an ordered society to which our world cannot as yet lay claim. Even such a society is not inherently pacific, since it usually comes into being and always maintains itself through some play of force; and all its civil ordinances are tainted with murder. If enough people join in crime, that crime becomes a revolution; and every war is an extension of civil revolution,

I

which, if it be successful, next imposes its own law; and whether that law is good or bad must be settled on other than legal grounds.

Why, then, are we at war? Many different answers might be, with some show of reason, offered. But Great Britain was, in its essence, its soul, forced sooner or later to oppose the tyrannic brutalities of the Hitlerian challenge. This is a simple human opposition in the realm of eternal values independent of any ' justice ' as to territorial boundaries, any League of Nations agreements, or any possible responsibility of our own statesmen for the rise of Hitler; and it is an opposition looking not back, but forward. When Mr. Chamberlain spoke of ' this wild beast that has sprung at us out of his lair ', his very phrase was symptomatic of our uncertainties. For it was not, strictly speaking, true. I am reminded of Saint George, who went out to slay a dragon, and has been honoured for it ever since. Let us admit frankly that, when the hour struck, we declared war on Hitler.

A preacher in Canterbury Cathedral once observed that Hitler's young armies were driven on by a fanatic belief which we might envy. But their faith, though powerful and sincere, remains wholly pagan. Germany appears deliberately to have fostered and used the beast within man, while dark presences, like the Weird Women in Shakespeare's *Macbeth*, have attended the adventure, lending it, for a while, their aid. But have we, on our side, no comparable strength? No purer magic to set against those dark and blood-stained demons? Germany reiterates the rights of her future. But have we, in our turn, no destiny? Some new creative faith is needed.

Perhaps we are right not to assert that we are fighting directly and only for Christ. We are, I think, sometimes too ready to acknowledge former errors and failings, though that very willingness holds a value nations of lesser experience misunderstand. Let us, however, be rightly humble, with a humility Christ Himself, knowing the baffling contradictions of our existence, would respect. He did not legislate directly for nations; but nevertheless on England, as nowhere else, falls the burden, though as yet dimly recognised, of tuning nations to His will. Moreover—and this appears to be even harder—on us, eventually, will be laid the compulsion of confessing, among ourselves and before the world, that this appointed task is ours, whatever dangers, hatred, or ridicule may be incurred. Meanwhile, we have for four years been fighting, alone or in partnership, the reptilian dragon-forces of unregenerate, and therefore unshaped and inhuman, instinct, energies breathing fire and slaughter across Europe, because such is our destiny, asserted by our own time-honoured national symbol, Saint George, the dragon-slayer, whose name our present sovereign bears; and we should first search out that destiny not in platitudes of half-belief nor any reasonings of our own fabrication, but where alone it rests authentic, in the great heritage we possess of English letters, the greatest accumulation of national prophecy, outside the Old Testament, that the world has seen; where the soul of England, which is her essential sovereignty, speaks clearly— in Shakespeare, Milton, Pope, Byron, Blake, Wordsworth, Tennyson, Hardy, and many more.* I offer no new analysis, but a new source of power; no historic reminder, but a prophetic insight. If ever a new Messiah is to come, he will come, says the greatest of all American writers, Herman Melville, in the name of Shakespeare. We need expect no Messiah, but we might, at this hour, turn to Shakespeare, a national prophet if ever there was one, concerned deeply with the royal soul of England. That royalty has direct Christian and chivalric affinities. Shakespeare's life-work might be characterised as expanding, through a series of great plays, the one central legend of Saint George and the Dragon. It would be well to face and accept our destiny in the names both of Shakespeare and of Saint George, the patron saint of our literature and nation.

* My reading of Milton's national assertion appears in *Chariot of Wrath*, Faber & Faber, 1942. For a similar approach to Tennyson, see *The Times, Literary Supplement*, 10 Oct., 1942.

ROSES AT WAR

I AIM to show what reserves for the refuelling of national confidence exist in Shakespeare's poetry. I shall refer briefly to
most of the plays without assuming first-hand knowledge of them.
I ask in return that my readers should attend carefully to each and
every quotation. If something must be skipped, skip my comments, which serve mainly to introduce and give contemporary
impact to a series of great passages.

Shakespeare wrote at a time when, after centuries of civil war,
England first became nationally self-conscious. Much, more perhaps than in any other nation, was compressed into that new,
English, consciousness. Diverse tendencies of medieval religion,
baronial aristocracy, middle-class trading and industry, and
peasant labour, which had before owned various allegiances either
outside England or to some lesser authority within our island,
fuse, after a preparatory period of civil and international conflict,
into a new whole. Henceforward England functions as England,
with a new sense of sovereignty, a new church, a new national
allegiance. That is how the Renaissance and Reformation affect,
or rather create, the England we know. The voice of the new
nation is Shakespeare.

His historical plays are mainly studies of internal disorder during the centuries leading to the England of Elizabeth. Shakespeare's thinking functions continually in terms of order. His
early love-tragedy, *Romeo and Juliet*, is more than a love-story
alone, as its prologue shows, being rather a love-story thrown into
sharp relation with, and finally serving to heal, civil discord.
Often in reading Shakespearian drama we do well to expand its
obvious content, to put world-affairs for the turbulences of state,
and modern nations, or parties, for separate persons. Well-known
works will then start up into sudden and fresh relief, with new,
because contemporary, meanings. The issues troubling Europe
to-day are here in embryo; and the desire for world-order which

4

fabricated the League of Nations is an expansion of a desire pulsing throughout Shakespeare.

Shakespeare's histories cannot be rightly understood without a reading of his earliest historical work, the three parts of *King Henry VI*. Part I, the least important, is mainly concerned with wars in France, Talbot playing the role of national hero and less than justice being done to Joan of Arc. Parts II and III are more important. These dramatise the Wars of the Roses, staging bitter animosities and bloody acts. Shakespeare here resembles his wild contemporary Christopher Marlowe; but though the events are Marlovian, the treatment is not. From the start there is a firm consciousness that brutality is brutal. We are reminded how heinous a sin it is to murder and rob, or to wrong virgin, orphan, or widow:

> Who can be bound by any solemn vow
> To do a murderous deed, to rob a man,
> To force a spotless virgin's chastity,
> To reave the orphan of his patrimony,
> To wring the widow from her custom'd right,
> And have no other reason for this wrong
> But that he was bound by a solemn oath?
>
> (*2 Henry VI*, V. i. 184.)

There is a basic sense of moral law:

> What stronger breastplate than a heart untainted!
> Thrice is he arm'd that hath his quarrel just,
> And he but naked, though lock'd up in steel,
> Whose conscience with injustice is corrupted.
>
> (*2 Henry VI*, III. ii. 232.)

But more significant than any ethic is the prevailing tone of piteous human feeling countering the ruthless savagery. The pathetic Henry VI, himself a weakling, watches a battle (*3 Henry VI*, II. v). First enters a 'son that hath killed his father, with the dead body'; next 'a father that hath killed his son'. Each in turn proceeds to plunder his prize, only to be brought up against the horror of his act. 'Pardon me, God, I knew not what I did!' cries one; and the other, 'O pity, God, this miserable age!' The king himself comments:

> Woe above woe! grief more than common grief!
> O that my death would stay these ruthful deeds!

> O, pity, pity, gentle heaven, pity !
> The red rose and the white are on his face,
> The fatal colours of our striving houses :
> The one his purple blood right well resembles ;
> The other his pale cheeks, methinks, presenteth ;
> Wither one rose, and let the other flourish ;
> If you contend, a thousand lives must wither.
>
> (II. v. 94.)

'The red rose and the white are on his face ' : it is as though blood were at war with flesh.   Civil war is shown as paradoxical and self-condemned, and no great imagination is to-day needed to expand the condemnation.   War makes of men, and women too, beasts.   Here is cruel Margaret, Henry's fierce queen, depicted for us :

> O tiger's heart wrapp'd in a woman's hide !
> How could'st thou drain the life-blood of the child,
> To bid the father wipe his eyes withal,
> And yet be seen to bear a woman's face ?
> Women are soft, mild, pitiful, and flexible ;
> Thou stern, obdurate, flinty, rough, remorseless.
>
> (3 Henry VI, I. iv. 137.)

Continually the savage actions of man are characterised in bestial terms.

The greatest things in these two plays arise from an over-powering sense of revulsion against insensate brutality :

> O, let the vile world end,
> And the premised flames of the last day
> Knit heaven and earth together !
> Now let the general trumpet blow his blast,
> Particularities and petty sounds
> To cease !   Wast thou ordain'd, dear father,
> To lose thy youth in peace, and to achieve
> The silver livery of advised age,
> And, in thy reverence and thy chair-days, thus
> To die in ruffian battle ?   Even at this sight
> My heart is turn'd to stone : and while 'tis mine,
> It shall be stony.
>
> (2 Henry VI, V. ii. 40.)

Shakespeare's poetry becomes more various and subtle, but, given a choice occasion, it already here achieves a maximum impact.

Each person is a unit of passionate energy and the poetry blazes. Single lines start up in compacted force, as

> Mine eyes should sparkle like the beaten flint
> (*2 Henry VI*, III. ii. 317.)

and

> We set the axe to thy usurping root
> (*3 Henry VI*, II. ii. 165.)

and

> That stain'd their fetlocks in his smoking blood
> (*3 Henry VI*, II. iii. 21.)

See how the impressions range over the human, animal, vegetable, and mineral creation, stung to life by each, making contact with the springs of existence. It is this which has caused critics to regard Shakespeare less as a literary artist than as a force of nature.

It has often been urged that a young man straight from Warwickshire could not have learnt so soon to speak with the accents of nobility; but it would be equally reasonable to grumble that the grand persons of *Henry VI* cannot open their mouths at a passionate moment without loading their speech with vivid analogies from nature. Here—as later in *Coriolanus*—the many analogies point us to an especially clear contrast of beasts of prey and gentle creatures; wolves, foxes, kites against lambs, chickens and partridges; or even caterpillars and leaves (*2 Henry VI*, III. i. 90). Many of the references show first-hand experience. Here is one:

> as I have seen a swan
> With bootless labour swim against the tide
> And spend her strength with over-matching waves . . .
> (*3 Henry VI*, I. iv. 19.)

And here another:

> Or as the snake, roll'd in a flowering bank,
> With shining checker'd slough, doth sting a child
> That for the beauty thinks it excellent . . .
> (*2 Henry VI*, III. i. 228.)

There is a quivering perception of animal suffering, seeing a lion's prey 'that trembles under his devouring paws' (*3 Henry VI*, I. iii. 13) and the 'trembling' wings of a bird 'limed in a bush' and now afraid to alight (*3 Henry VI*, V. vi. 14). There are mild birds defending their young with ferocity, and pathetic birds, prisoned in cages and singing there; and the ' fearful ' hare flying from greyhounds whose eyes sparkle with wrath (*3 Henry VI*, II. v. 130). All creation seems at work preying, slaughtering, devouring:

> And as the butcher takes away the calf,
> And binds the wretch, and beats it when it strays,
> Bearing it to the bloody slaughter-house,
> Even so remorseless have they borne him hence;
> And as the dam runs lowing up and down,
> Looking the way her harmless young one went,
> And can do nought but wail her darling's loss,
> Even so myself bewails good Gloucester's case.
>
> (*2 Henry VI*, III. i. 210.)

Man's warring flowers only too naturally from a universe apparently patterned of blood. And yet we are continually pointed back to the unnaturalness of cruelty. The paradox is left unresolved.

With such analogies the dramatic presentation of civil war is over and over again loaded. It is, indeed, interesting to observe the exact point in the sequence where they start to cluster the page; after that, they never leave it, and are supported by continual references to the seasons and its fruits, warmth and cold, and the drama of the skies.

This vital feeling of beauty and agony within the very texture of physical existence naturally extends to a vivid awareness of human physique too, the face especially, as in the lines

> He knits his brow and shows an angry eye
> (*2 Henry VI*, III. i. 15.)

> Beaufort's red sparkling eyes blab his heart's malice
> (*2 Henry VI*, III. i. 154.)

and

> Look pale as primrose with blood-drinking sighs
> (*2 Henry VI*, III. ii. 63.)

or so fine a couplet as

> Upon thy eyeballs murderous tyranny
> Sits in grim majesty, to fright the world.
> (*2 Henry VI*, III. ii. 49.)

The tragic events are presented with a vivid physical realism:

> See how the blood is settled in his face.
> Oft have I seen a timely-parted ghost,
> Of ashy semblance, meagre, pale, and bloodless,
> Being all descended to the labouring heart;
> Who, in the conflict that it holds with death,
> Attracts the same for aidance 'gainst the enemy;
> Which with the heart there cools and ne'er returneth
> To blush and beautify the cheek again.
> But see, his face is black and full of blood,
> His eye-balls further out than when he lived,
> Staring full ghastly like a strangled man;
> His hair uprear'd, his nostrils stretch'd with struggling;
> His hands abroad display'd, as one that grasp'd
> And tugg'd for life and was by strength subdued:
> Look, on the sheets his hair, you see, is sticking;
> His well-proportion'd beard made rough and rugged,
> Like to the summer's corn by tempest lodg'd.
>
> (*2 Henry VI*, III. ii. 160.)

The impact may, as here, be gruesome; or it may come alive with a strong, maternal piteousness for a beautiful body broken and gashed, seeing a slaughtered youth as a ' tender spray ' ' sweetly ' sprung from his ' princely father ' (*3 Henry VI*, II. vi. 47–51). The blood of the slain is felt, by relative or supporter, as a rich, sweet, potent, yet piteous thing. Neither side has any monopoly of these images: the terrible Margaret can be as pathetic as anyone.

The horrors of war are carefully dramatised through a series of individual deaths; those of Humphrey, Duke of Gloucester; Clifford; Rutland; Suffolk; Warwick; Prince Edward, and finally Henry VI himself. The succession of personal griefs gives a dramatic poignance no impressions of massed warfare could attain. The more generalised feeling that results is phrased by King Henry in a lovely speech of Shakespearian pastoralism:

> O God! methinks it were a happy life,
> To be no better than a homely swain;
> To sit upon a hill, as I do now,
> To carve out dials quaintly, point by point,
> Thereby to see the minutes how they run,
> How many make the hour full complete;
> How many hours bring about the day;
> How many days will finish up the year;

B

How many years a mortal man may live.
When this is known, then to divide the times :
So many hours must I tend my flock;
So many hours must I take my rest;
So many hours must I contemplate;
So many hours must I sport myself;
So many days my ewes have been with young;
So many weeks ere the poor fools will ean;
So many years ere I shall shear the fleece :
So minutes, hours, days, months, and years,
Pass'd over to the end they were created,
Would bring white hairs unto a quiet grave.
Ah ! what a life were this ! how sweet ! how lovely !
Gives not the hawthorn-bush a sweeter shade
To shepherds looking on their silly sheep,
Than doth a rich embroider'd canopy
To kings that fear their subjects' treachery ?
O, yes, it doth; a thousand-fold it doth.
And to conclude, the shepherd's homely curds,
His cold thin drink out of his leather bottle,
His wonted sleep under a fresh tree's shade,
All which secure and sweetly he enjoys,
Is far beyond a prince's delicates,
His viands sparkling in a golden cup,
His body couched in a curious bed,
When care, mistrust, and treason wait on him.

                              (3 *Henry VI*, II. v. 21.)

This is the central comment of the whole, just as the King himself, in his unworldly, generous weakness, is the central figure.

Much of Shakespeare's future work is implicit in *Henry VI*, our thoughts being pointed variously ahead to other Histories, and greater plays like *Macbeth* and *Coriolanus*. The pity and the pastoralism are to run throughout his work; and so too is the keen sense of physical existence, in plant, animal, or man. But some things are not yet fully developed. In *Henry VI* we face a world of men and women violent, passionate, loyal, and pathetic. Frenzied actions make the victims' supporters stifle their natural instincts and commit more ruthless acts which turn more hearts to stone: it is a vicious circle and, like Europe to-day, they cannot get out of it. Though violent, they are, in a deeper sense, all strangely passive: they are at the mercy of circumstances and their uncontrolled selves. More—they inevitably end by handing over the control of their country to the tyrannous Richard III, who explicitly renounces all the 'soft laws' of 'nature' (*3 Henry VI*, III. ii. 154) with a considered philosophy of egotism, saying 'I am myself alone' (*3 Henry VI*, V. vi. 83). He at least makes some sense of this chaos—for awhile.

From now on, a new strength is to dominate Shakespeare's work. More, his people themselves are henceforth greater. They may be either good or evil, but they exist in a new dimension. The people of *Henry VI* are marvellous creatures; but they are just that—creatures. They are neither good nor evil. Richard III, Faulconbridge in *King John*, Richard II, Henry IV, Hotspur and Falstaff, Henry V—all are variously, in a new sense, great; so, we may add, are many of the people that surround them. What is this greatness?

I shall not attempt to define it here. It has much, very much, to do with Shakespeare's rooted naturalism and refusal to make any distinction between man and the rest of God's creation, his ability 'to see how God in all his creatures works' (*2 Henry VI*, II. i. 7). That gives him his insight into human energies and his trust in man as man. For the rest, its symptoms, irrespective of ethical good or evil, are dignity and courage; the will to wrestle with a chaotic universe and make something of it; and spiritual depth. With this grows a new feeling for kingly office, and for England, as a nation. The greater persons to follow are all, good or bad, dedicated men; in a wider sense, the plays are dedicated plays—expressions of the poet's mind at grips with the problem of human discord and willing the mastery of its horrors.

III

SAINT GEORGE FOR ENGLAND

WE are now to glance shortly at Shakespeare's better known historical plays. Most of them take him back earlier than the reign of Henry VI, but they express none the less a developing plan.

In *King John*, a good play to start with, Shakespeare studies that important reign during which England is felt groping towards independence. The nation's relationship to the continent, and especially the Church of Rome, is subtly presented. About this I shall have more to say later. Here we may notice Shakespeare's early feeling for England's true strength, dependent on two things, which are really the same, the coming home of her revolted barons, that is, unity; and truth to herself. This is our final speech:

> This England never did, nor never shall,
> Lie at the proud foot of a conqueror,
> But when it first did help to wound itself.
> Now these her princes are come home again,
> Come the three corners of the world in arms,
> And we shall shock them. Nought shall make us rue,
> If England to itself do rest but true.
>
> (V. vii. 112.)

This is spoken by the Bastard, Faulconbridge, the bluff, humorous, critical, warm-hearted and typically English son of Richard Coeur-de-Lion. Compare Hastings' words in *Henry VI*:

Hastings : Why, knows not Montague that of itself
England is safe if true within itself?

Montague : Yes; but the safer when 'tis back'd with France.

Hastings : 'Tis better using France than trusting France:
Let us be back'd with God and with the seas
Which he hath given for fence impregnable,
And with their helps only defend ourselves;
In them and in ourselves our safety lies.

(*3 Henry VI*, IV. i. 39.)

Faulconbridge's faith, to return to *King John*, is not lightly held; for he speaks earlier what is as trenchant a criticism of international bargaining as you will anywhere find, England being one

of the parties criticised. The passage is difficult, but recent
criticisms of 'appeasement' make it lively contemporary reading.

> Mad world ! mad kings ! mad composition !
> John, to stop Arthur's title in the whole,
> Hath willingly departed with a part :
> And France, whose armour conscience buckled on,
> Whom zeal and charity brought to the field
> As God's own soldier, rounded in the ear
> With that same purpose-changer, that sly devil,
> That broker, that still breaks the pate of faith,
> That daily break-vow, he that wins of all,
> Of kings, of beggars, old men, young men, maids,
> Who, having no external thing to lose
> But the word ' maid ', cheats the poor maid of that,
> That smooth-faced gentleman, tickling Commodity,
> Commodity, the bias of the world,
> The world, who of itself is peised well,
> Made to run even upon even ground,
> Till this advantage, this vile-drawing bias,
> This sway of motion, this Commodity,
> Makes it take head from all indifferency,
> From all direction, purpose, course, intent :
> And this same bias, this Commodity,
> This bawd, this broker, this all-changing word,
> Clapp'd on the outward eye of fickle France,
> Hath drawn him from his own determined aid,
> From a resolved and honourable war,
> To a most base and vile-concluded peace.
> And why rail I on this Commodity ?
> But for because he hath not woo'd me yet :
> Not that I have the power to clutch my hand
> When his fair angels would salute my palm ;
> But for my hand, as unattempted yet,
> Like a poor beggar, raileth on the rich.
> Well, whiles I am a beggar, I will rail
> And say there is no sin but to be rich ;
> And being rich, my virtue then shall be
> To say there is no vice but beggary.
> Since kings break faith upon Commodity,
> Gain, be my lord, for I will worship thee.

(II. i. 561.)

Papal intrigue and national rivalry, hard-headed loyalty and semi-
virtuous treachery, all jostle each other. Sometimes, as when
Faulconbridge is shocked and baffled by young Arthur's death

(IV. iii. 139–59), a speech is poignant with an emotion touching
our own uncertainties. But see how such uncertainties are next
rebuked by Faulconbridge, urging John to be resolute in face of
foreign invasion in terms finely applicable to England, as a whole,
to-day:

> Be great in act, as you have been in thought;
> Let not the world see fear and sad distrust
> Govern the motion of a kingly eye:
> Be stirring as the time; be fire with fire;
> Threaten the threatener, and outface the brow
> Of bragging horror: so shall inferior eyes,
> That borrow their behaviours from the great,
> Grow great by your example and put on
> The dauntless spirit of resolution.
> Away! and glister like the god of war
> When he intendeth to become the field:
> Show boldness and aspiring confidence.
> What! shall they seek the lion in his den
> And fright him there? and make him tremble there?
> O! let it not be said.
>
> (V. i. 45.)

That infectious fervour is, nevertheless, countered by another
Shakespearian reminder:

> O nation, that thou couldst remove!
> That Neptune's arms, who clippeth thee about,
> Would bear thee from the knowledge of thyself,
> And gripple thee unto a pagan shore;
> Where these two Christian armies might combine
> The blood of malice in a vein of league,
> And not to spend it so unneighbourly!
>
> (V. ii. 33.)

Shakespeare knows, well enough, the un-Christian nature of war,
and the confusion is at last ended by the Pope's legate. The peace
is thus forwarded by John's religious submission. But Cardinal
Pandulph is an intriguer like the rest, and the manly voice of
Faulconbridge has the final say, speaking only of England.

England must be true to herself: that is the burden of Shakespeare's unsentimental patriotism. A characteristic blend of sharp
criticism with patriotic fervour is compressed within a single
speech of what was probably a slightly earlier play, *Richard II*.
We may apply it to our own class differences of recent years;

especially the wrongs of capitalist indulgence in England's social
history, wrongs not primarily against another class, but rather
against the innate royalty of the nation from which all classes hold
their rights. Old John of Gaunt, seeing himself as ' a prophet
new inspired ', grieves in quavering, repetitive accents at the spend-
thrift king and the selfish prostitution of his country's soul to an
immediate, monetary, gain:

> This royal throne of kings, this scepter'd isle,
> This earth of majesty, this seat of Mars,
> This other Eden, demi-paradise ;
> This fortress built by Nature for herself
> Against infection and the hand of war ;
> This happy breed of men, this little world,
> This precious stone set in the silver sea,
> Which serves it in the office of a wall,
> Or as a moat defensive to a house,
> Against the envy of less happier lands ;
> This blessed plot, this earth, this realm, this England,
> This nurse, this teeming womb of royal kings,
> Fear'd by their breed and famous by their birth,
> Renowned for their deeds as far from home,
> For Christian service and true chivalry,
> As is the sepulchre in stubborn Jewry
> Of the world's ransom, blessed Mary's Son ;
> This land of such dear souls, this dear, dear land,
> Dear for her reputation through the world,
> Is now leased out, I die pronouncing it,
> Like to a tenement or pelting farm :
> England, bound in with the triumphant sea,
> Whose rocky shore beats back the envious siege
> Of watery Neptune, is now bound in with shame,
> With inky blots and rotten parchment bonds :
> That England, that was wont to conquer others,
> Hath made a shameful conquest of itself.
> Ah, would the scandal vanish with my life,
> How happy then were my ensuing death.
>
> (II. i. 40.)

How illogical, to our way of thinking, seems this emphasis on
kings; but it is the royal soul of England that Shakespeare is defin-
ing, just as the word ' prophet ', used to introduce the passage, has,
poetically, a deeper content than the dramatic context alone would
suggest. The speech clearly transcends its supposed historic
setting, and seems, indeed, more suited to our time than to Shake-

speare's. It is prophetic of England's then scarcely apparent
destiny; and when our reformers speak with such an accent,
urging the wrongs of big business in words of that royal calibre,
or take such a speech as this for their text, men will listen with a
new keenness. Our ' left ' thinking has remained sterile, because
merely rationalist, and therefore soul-less. Even when most
constructive it has lacked the glow of a creative faith.

Such a conception is this golden thread in England's story
which we are now considering. The Crown symbolises the
nation's soul-life, which is also the greater self of each subject.
In Shakespeare's human kings we watch different persons under-
taking that supreme responsibility; and we can view each personal
king as a prototype of national action, as England herself, fulfilling
or falsifying her destiny.

We have seen how Shakespeare's first historical study gave us
the three parts of *Henry VI*, where the swaying internal discords
of York and Lancaster, the Wars of the Roses, work to a conclusion; but that conclusion is a bitter one, throwing up, from
this hell-cauldron of bloodshed and hate, a new danger in the
satanic figure of Richard, duke of Gloucester.

Richard III is a fascinating play and Richard himself has much
in common with Hitler. His first soliloquy shows a sense of
inferiority due to his deformed stature: one may notice in passing
that Tamburlaine was lame and dictators are usually small men.
He chooses villainy, now wars are over, as a compensation for lack
of sexual appeal and the normal graces of peace. One can point
to Hitler's years of hardship and failure and the absence of any
woman's love in his life-story. True, Richard woos Anne
successfully; but here again his almost absurdly theatrical reversal
of her loathing, due both to his crimes and appearance, with his
ability to play precisely the same trick later on another woman,
may remind us forcibly of Hitler's successful technique of repeated
deception. Richard is a master of hypocrisy corresponding closely
to the propaganda of Hitler's regime; both appearing to take an
almost humorous delight in embarrassing their enemies by playing
on those Christian values they nevertheless thoroughly intend
themselves to repudiate, seeing supposed goodness as the attribute
of weaklings. Notice how Richard swears continually by his

favourite, Saint Paul.   Richard, like Hitler, kicks away the ladder
on which he rose, Buckingham corresponding to Röhm.   The
good, or rather the less bad, men surrounding the hero certainly
seem nonentities in comparison with the central superman.   They
belong still to the world of *Henry VI*, highly emotional, piteous,
unprincipled, and finally enslaved.   Richard is a greater than
they: he is master of his own fate.   We may recall the many
weaknesses in Great Britain and Europe that have made the
Hitlerian adventure possible.

Richard's fate is, however, terrible enough.   He suffers from
' timorous ' dreams (IV. i. 84); his soliloquies in *Henry VI* show
that he had from the first a clear conception of the gentler values;
and at the play's close he sees ghosts.   Under Richmond—whose
role of saviour was foretold in *Henry VI*—a righteous force opposes
his tyrannic rule, and on the eve of battle the souls of all his victims
enter his tent to pronounce doom on their murderer and bless
Richmond's sword.   As these dim figures form round the sleep-
ing Richard, we can feel the various countries Germany has
temporarily enslaved speaking with their voices:

> Dream on, dream on, of bloody deeds and death :
> Fainting, despair; despairing, yield thy breath !
>
> (V. iii. 172.)

Each ghost turns also to Richmond, assuring to his sword an
angelic strength.   Hitler has played out his story on a vaster
scale, but the spiritual issues involved are similar; for he, too,
sees ghosts and knows, according to Hermann Rauschning's *Hitler
Speaks*, certain frenzied fears directly comparable with Richard's.
He wakes at night with ' convulsive shrieks ', and on one such
occasion was found shouting, ' He! He! He's been here! '—
his lips blue and sweat streaming down his face.   This is Shakespeare's version, playing on the enigma of conscience :

> Give me another horse, bind up my wounds !
> Have mercy, Jesu !—Soft ! I did but dream.
> O coward conscience, how dost thou afflict me !
> The lights burn blue.   It is now dead midnight.
> Cold fearful drops stand on my trembling flesh.
> What do I fear ? myself ? there's none else by :
> Richard loves Richard; that is, I am I.
> Is there a murderer here ?   No.   Yes, I am :

Then fly. What, from myself? Great reason why:
Lest I revenge. What, myself upon myself?
Alack, I love myself. Wherefore? for any good
That I myself have done unto myself?
O, no! alas, I rather hate myself
For hateful deeds committed by myself!
I am a villain: yet I lie, I am not.
Fool, of thyself speak well: fool, do not flatter.
My conscience hath a thousand several tongues,
And every tongue brings in a several tale,
And every tale condemns me for a villain.
Perjury, perjury, in the high'st degree;
Murder, stern murder, in the direst degree;
All several sins, all used in each degree,
Throng to the bar, crying all 'Guilty! guilty!'
I shall despair. There is no creature loves me;
And if I die, no soul will pity me.
Nay, wherefore should they, since that I myself
Find in myself no pity to myself?
Methought the souls of all that I had murder'd
Came to my tent, and every one did threat
To-morrow's vengeance on the head of Richard.

(V. iii. 178.)

Something deep in Richard already sides with his accusers, but his daylight will remains impregnable. When he recovers and asserts ' Our strong arms be our conscience, swords our law ' (V. iii. 312) we recognise the philosophy. So in demonic pride he goes to his bloody end :

Let us to't pell-mell;
If not to heaven, then hand in hand to hell!

(V. iii. 313.)

True, we cannot deny to Richard our semi-reluctant admiration. Though wicked, he remains great.

He is, in mind and body, deformed. His victims compare him to beasts, ugly, reptilian, and dangerous. He is called a dog, a ' bottled spider ', a ' poisonous bunch-back'd toad ', an ' elvish-mark'd, abortive, rooting hog ' (I. iii. 216–46), a ' hell-hound that doth hunt us all to death ' (IV. iv. 48), a ' cacodemon ' (I. iii. 144). Such evil is often in Shakespeare felt as inhuman and bestial; it is—or should be—un-English; and the central symbolism to which Shakespeare's English warriors regularly appeal before battle is Saint George, the dragon-vanquisher. In *Henry VI*

Talbot in a speech of national daring boasts he will celebrate
Saint George's feast in France, and in the civil warfare of the
second and third parts both sides cry on God and Saint George
before battle.   Now here both Richard and Richmond do the
same; both lay claim to Saint George's protection.   But can
Richard properly do such a thing ?   Once earlier, when he swore
by his ' George ', ' garter ', and ' crown ', his interlocutor answered
crisply, ' Profaned, dishonour'd, and the third usurp'd ' (IV. iv.
368).   Whatever courage he may show, Richard cannot with
reason appeal to Saint George.   The whole play is against him.
He is himself far nearer to the dragon, and is therefore driven up
against a logical paradox:

> Our ancient word of courage, fair Saint George,
> Inspire us with the spleen of fiery dragons !
>
> (V. iii. 350.)

It is the dragon part of the emblem with which he recognises
personal kinship, nor does he, like Richmond, couple the Saint's
name with ' God '.   He is, in fact, himself the Dragon.

Here is Richmond's address to his soldiers:

> Yet remember this,
> God and our good cause fight upon our side ;
> The prayers of holy saints and wronged souls,
> Like high-rear'd bulwarks, stand before our faces ;
> Richard except, those whom we fight against
> Had rather have us win than him they follow.
> For what is he they follow ? truly, gentlemen,
> A bloody tyrant and a homicide ;
> One rais'd in blood, and one in blood establish'd ;
> One that made means to come by what he hath,
> And slaughter'd those that were the means to help him ;
> A base foul stone, made precious by the foil
> Of England's chair, where he is falsely set ;
> One that hath ever been God's enemy.
> Then, if you fight against God's enemy,
> God will in justice ward you as his soldiers ;
> If you do sweat to put a tyrant down,
> You sleep in peace, the tyrant being slain ;
> If you do fight against your country's foes,
> Your country's fat shall pay your pains the hire ;
> If you do fight in safeguard of your wives,
> Your wives shall welcome home the conquerors ;

> If you do free your children from the sword,
> Your children's children quit it in your age.
> Then, in the name of God and all these rights,
> Advance your standards, draw your willing swords.
>
>   (V. iii. 240.)

England is felt as ejecting from her own constitution, as a foul
disease, the tyrannous and bloody thing she has so often since
opposed in other nations; and the play ends with some great lines
by Richmond on the peace won by his victorious arm.   But that is
not the whole story: for Richard's address to his army wielded
also a burly patriotism of its own: something of British virility
(resembling—as Prof. John Laird has observed—that of Faulconbridge) is certainly in him.   Shakespeare in this early play saw
deep into both the greatness and the short-lived success of such
ambition as Richard's, and was the better able, through the following series, *King John* included, to hammer out his conception of
how an English king—that is, how England—should behave.
After writing the three parts of *Henry VI* and *Richard III*, having
brought the historic sequence almost to his own century, he goes
farther back historically, though with an advancing conception.
King John I have noticed and shall return to; the remaining four
plays, *Richard II*, the two parts of *Henry IV*, and *Henry V*, com-
plete, for the time being, his structure.

In *Richard II* we are shown the exact opposite of our last
Richard.   Here we have a weak, inefficient, luxury-loving king.
He fairly accurately represents a tendency clear in our recent
history, and, as I have argued, John of Gaunt's prophetic denuncia-
tion in terms of ' rotten parchment bonds ' registers to-day.   The
King tries to avoid trouble and remove those ready

> To wake our peace, which in our country's cradle
> Draws the sweet infant breath of gentle sleep,
>
>   (I. iii. 132.)

—who would involve his land in the ' dreadful bray ' of trumpets
and ' grating shock of wrathful iron arms' (I. iii. 136).   He
returns from his Irish expedition to meet rebellion in England,
and his speech bursts into flower:

> I weep for joy
> To stand upon my kingdom once again.
> Dear earth, I do salute thee with my hand,

Though rebels wound thee with their horses' hoofs :
As a long-parted mother with her child
Plays fondly with her tears and smiles in meeting,
So, weeping, smiling, greet I thee, my earth,
And do thee favour with my royal hands.
Feed not thy sovereign's foe, my gentle earth,
Nor with thy sweets comfort his ravenous sense ;
But let thy spiders, that suck up thy venom,
And heavy-gaited toads lie in their way,
Doing annoyance to the treacherous feet
Which with usurping steps do trample thee :
Yield stinging nettles to mine enemies ;
And when they from thy bosom pluck a flower,
Guard it, I pray thee, with a lurking adder,
Whose double tongue may with a mortal touch
Throw death upon thy sovereign's enemies.
Mock not my senseless conjuration, lords :
This earth shall have a feeling and these stones
Prove armed soldiers, ere her native king
Shall falter under foul rebellion's arms.

(III. ii. 4.)

Notice how closely are England's natural sweets in Shakespeare
entwined with her human and political integrity. Richard's
followers urge him to action, accuse him of enjoying too great a
' security ' while his enemies grow powerful. He answers:

Discomfortable cousin ! know'st thou not
That when the searching eye of heaven is hid
Behind the globe, and lights the lower world,
Then thieves and robbers range abroad unseen
In murders and in outrage boldly here ;
But when from under this terrestrial ball
He fires the proud tops of the eastern pines
And darts his light through every guilty hole,
Then murders, treasons, and detested sins,
The cloak of night being pluck'd from off their backs,
Stand bare and naked, trembling at themselves ?
So when this thief, this traitor, Bolingbroke,
Who all this while hath revell'd in the night,
Whilst we were wandering with the antipodes,
Shall see us rising in our throne, the east,
His treasons will sit blushing in his face,
Not able to endure the sight of day,
But self-affrighted tremble at his sin.
Not all the water in the rough rude sea
Can wash the balm from an anointed king ;

> The breath of worldly men cannot depose
> The deputy elected by the Lord.
> For every man that Bolingbroke hath press'd
> To lift shrewd steel against our golden crown,
> God for his Richard hath in heavenly pay
> A glorious angel : then, if angels fight,
> Weak men must fall, for heaven still guards the right.
>
> (III. ii. 36.)

We can rely too confidently on Heaven's guardian might. Richard does so; and we should consider carefully the opposition Shakespeare draws of confidence and disillusion. In reading such a speech we must (i) respect the essence of divine authority as existent in its own right, although (ii) we are aware of Richard's unsuitability for his high office. We can next make a cross-reference to Great Britain as a nation: for she has, as her greatest poets are aware, a destiny which she is in continual danger of discrediting, whilst nevertheless half expecting it to do for her what she will not do for herself.

Richard's assurance is at first too glib and swiftly reversed to a defeatist resignation:

> No matter where; of comfort no man speak :
> Let's talk of graves, of worms and epitaphs . . .
> Our lands, our lives, and all, are Bolingbroke's,
> And nothing can we call our own but death . . .
>
> (III. ii. 144.)

Richard now recognises that he is a man only: ' I live with bread like you, feel want, taste grief, need friends ' (III. ii. 175). But, as the clouds gather, he grows in stature—it is a way all Shakespeare's tragic heroes have—and his tone grows darker and richer:

> We are amazed; and thus long have we stood
> To watch the fearful bending of thy knee,
> Because we thought ourself thy lawful king :
> And if we be, how dare thy joints forget
> To pay their awful duty to our presence?
> If we be not, show us the hand of God
> That hath dismiss'd us from our stewardship;
> For well we know, no hand of blood and bone
> Can gripe the sacred handle of our sceptre,
> Unless he do profane, steal, or usurp.
> And though you think that all, as you have done,
> Have torn their souls by turning them from us,

And we are barren and bereft of friends;
Yet know, my master, God omnipotent
Is mustering in his clouds on our behalf
Armies of pestilence; and they shall strike
Your children yet unborn and unbegot,
That lift your vassal hands against my head,
And threat the glory of my precious crown.
Tell Bolingbroke—for yond methinks he is—
That every stride he makes upon my land
Is dangerous treason : he is come to open
The purple testament of bleeding war;
But ere the crown he looks for live in peace,
Ten thousand bloody crowns of mothers' sons
Shall ill become the flower of England's face,
Change the complexion of her maid-pale peace
To scarlet indignation, and bedew
Her pastures' grass with faithful English blood.

(III. iii. 72.)

Whatever we think of Richard, some sacred essence, at once pastoral and royal, is being wronged: in no play is Shakespeare's royalism so poetically explicit. Moreover, this prophecy will be, after his death, fulfilled, and Richard's warning is not, if a long view be taken, misplaced. Next he slips into a luxuriant mysticism that has its own beauty, though further emphasising his unsuitability for temporal office. But then again, when formally renouncing his crown, from height of a new tragic dignity, he denounces traitorous rebellion in scorching words, branding that ' heinous ' deed, the ' cracking ' of a sacred oath, with Heaven's curse, and comparing his tormentors to Judas and to Pilate, and himself to Christ; while including himself in his denunciation for the crime of having willingly undecked ' the pompous body of a king ' (IV. i. 162–242). Independent of any personal considerations whatsoever, some essential, superpersonal, sovereignty takes on mysterious, compelling, glistening presence.

Richard meets his death with a towering courage:

How now ! What means death in this rude assault ?
Villain, thine own hand yields thy death's instrument.
Go thou and fill another room in hell.
That hand shall burn in never-quenching fire
That staggers thus my person. Exton, thy fierce hand
Hath with the king's blood stain'd the king's own land.

(V. v. 106.)

He kills two of them before himself falling; and this is Shakespeare's weak king. We are a long way from Henry VI, and still farther from Marlowe's Edward II. Such innate royalty Marlowe never conceived.

Often Richard is compared to the sun; the sun, and Christ. The king is Christ's deputy on earth, and Richard should therefore have possessed something of nature's power. Richard III certainly had too much of the beast in him; but Richard II has too little; and when his queen and he part, she accuses of unmanly weakness one who should more properly be a ' lion ' and ' king of beasts ' (V. i. 34). His religious and tragic mysticism is poetically exquisite, but lacks practical relevance. Such is Shakespeare's judgment on a king—or country—that pursues reliance on divine sanctions, while lacking wholly that virility without which temporal affairs cannot be ordered, nor the realms of justice and love be rendered secure.

Though Richard may be wrong, revolution—the thought is Shakespearian—cannot exactly be right. In *Richard II* a discrepancy exists between true sovereignty and its exponent, leading to disaster. Richard's successor, Bolingbroke, now Henry IV, though a strong man, is worn down by civil disturbances:

> So shaken as we are, so wan with care,
> Find we a time for frighted peace to pant,
> And breathe short-winded accents of new broils
> To be commenc'd in stronds afar remote.
> No more the thirsty entrance of this soil
> Shall daub her lips with her own children's blood ;
> No more shall trenching war channel her fields,
> Nor bruise her flowerets with the armed hoofs
> Of hostile paces : those opposed eyes,
> Which, like the meteors of a troubled heaven,
> All of one nature, of one substance bred,
> Did lately meet in the intestine shock
> And furious close of civil butchery,
> Shall now, in mutual well-beseeming ranks,
> March all one way, and be no more oppos'd
> Against acquaintance, kindred, and allies :
> The edge of war, like an ill-sheathed knife,
> No more shall cut his master. Therefore, friends,
> As far as to the sepulchre of Christ—
> Whose soldier now, under whose blessed cross

We are impressed and engag'd to fight—
Forthwith a power of English shall we levy,
Whose arms were moulded in their mother's womb
To chase these pagans in those holy fields
Over whose acres walk'd those blessed feet
Which fourteen hundred years ago were nail'd
For our advantage on the bitter cross.

(*1 Henry IV*, I. i. 1.)

He wishes to cleanse his hands of Richard's blood by a Crusade, but disorder at home continues and his purpose fails. The two parts of *Henry IV* show a nation condemned to a slow agony of self-conflict, in which both sides bear guilt. Here we have the Archbishop of York characterised as a rebel:

You, lord archbishop,
Whose see is by a civil peace maintain'd,
Whose beard the silver hand of peace hath touch'd,
Whose learning and good letters peace hath tutor'd,
Whose white investments figure innocence,
The dove and very blessed spirit of peace,
Wherefore do you so ill translate yourself
Out of the speech of peace that bears such grace
Into the harsh and boisterous tongue of war;
Turning your books to greaves, your ink to blood,
Your pens to lances, and your tongue divine
To a loud trumpet and a point of war?

(*2 Henry IV*, IV. i. 41.)

And again:

My Lord of York, it better show'd with you,
When that your flock, assembled by the bell,
Encircled you to hear with reverence
Your exposition on the holy text
Than now to see you here an iron man,
Cheering a rout of rebels with your drum,
Turning the word to sword and life to death.

(*2 Henry IV*, IV. ii. 4.)

Shakespeare's Histories are rich with images of peace.

Henry is primarily a worried king, set half-way between Richard III and Richard II, with strength and weakness, determination and repentance, intermingling:

How many thousand of my poorest subjects
Are at this hour asleep! O sleep, O gentle sleep,

c

Nature's soft nurse, how have I frighted thee,
That thou no more wilt weigh my eyelids down,
And steep my senses in forgetfulness?
Why rather, sleep, liest thou in smoky cribs,
Upon uneasy pallets stretching thee,
And hush'd with buzzing night-flies to thy slumber,
Than in the perfumed chambers of the great,
Under the canopies of costly state,
And lull'd with sound of sweetest melody?
O thou dull god, why liest thou with the vile
In loathsome beds, and leavest the kingly couch
A watch-case or a common 'larum-bell?
Wilt thou upon the high and giddy mast
Seal up the ship-boy's eyes, and rock his brains
In cradle of the rude imperious surge,
And in the visitation of the winds,
Who take the ruffian billows by the top,
Curling their monstrous heads, and hanging them
With deafening clamour in the slippery clouds,
That, with the hurly, death itself awakes?
Canst thou, O partial sleep, give thy repose
To the wet sea-boy in an hour so rude,
And in the calmest and most stillest night,
With all appliances and means to boot,
Deny it to a king? Then happy low, lie down!
Uneasy lies the head that wears a crown.

                                    (*2 Henry IV*, III. i. 4.)

How inward is the Shakespearian intuition of sovereignty, disclosing, beneath the show and trappings of world-power, its bitterness and unrest Set beside this the barbaric, Hitlerian, Tamburlaine of Shakespeare's contemporary Marlowe:

A god is not so glorious as a king.
To ask and have; command and be obeyed. . . .

The contrast shows the spiritual depth of the Shakespearian and, I think, the more typically British, approach to power; Britain's success as a colonising force having derived from some such sense of responsible authority. King Henry's repeated intention of voyaging to the Holy Land to wash the guilt of Richard's blood from his hands is not consummated; but the humble reference of England's royal history to that higher court of justice and mercy overarching nations is important. I see this guilt-burdened king as a symbol of all secular authority, of any time or place.

Henry IV is, too, worried about his son, Hal, so dissolute in comparison with the rebel Hotspur, always thirsting for military honour. Hal deliberately idles away his time with Falstaff, the fat drunkard of philosophic humour and trenchant wit. In Hal Shakespeare is at work, throughout the two parts of *Henry IV*, in constructing an ideal English type, with even that streak of a politic worldly-wisdom not openly acknowledged, a high serious-ness unsuspected until the crucial moment reveals it, which appears hypocrisy to the continental mind. For Hal is to develop even-tually into the ideal king, Henry V. Shakespeare deliberately apprentices him to Falstaff, who grows out of his setting of noble rivalries and military prowess like a vast green cabbage from the flaring reds and blues and golden petalled faces of a flower-bed. Falstaff repudiates all heroisms. Here he is, before the battle:

> *Falstaff :* I would 'twere bed-time, Hal, and all well.
> *Prince :* Why, thou owest God a death.
>
> [*Exit.*]
> *Falstaff :* 'Tis not due yet; I would be loath to pay him before his day. What need I be so forward with him that calls not on me? Well, 'tis no matter; honour pricks me on. Yea, but how if honour prick me off when I come on? how then? Can honour set to a leg? no: or an arm? no: or take away the grief of a wound? no. Honour hath no skill in surgery, then? no. What is honour? a word. What is that word honour? air. A trim reckoning! Who hath it? he that died o' Wednesday. Doth he feel it? no. Doth he hear it? no. It is insensible, then? Yea, to the dead. But will it not live with the living? no. Why? detraction will not suffer it. Therefore I'll none of it. Honour is a mere scutcheon; and so ends my catechism.
>
> (*1 Henry IV*, V. i. 126.)

Later, on the field of battle, seeing, and perhaps turning over with his boot, Sir Walter Blunt's (probably ungraceful) dead body, he says, ' There's honour for you '. He expands that rough and burly common-sense in approaching kings and all their ways which we noticed in Faulconbridge to a general satire on martial heroism and all aristocratic valuation whatsoever, at one point even burlesquing the king himself in Hal's presence. The second part of *Henry IV*, a more bitter play than the first, presents a dastardly example of treachery in Prince John of Lancaster, a young man very neatly criticised by Falstaff; and here too Shake-

speare ably satirises the methods of the press-gangs. Falstaff's
comment on his ragamuffin army in Part I had an undertone of
bitterness:

> Tut, tut ; good enough to toss ; food for powder, food for powder ;
> they'll fill a pit as well as better : tush, man, mortal men, mortal men.
> (IV. ii. 72.)

It is, I think, a supreme stroke of Shakespeare to have appren-
ticed his hero-to-be, Henry V, to such a tutor as Falstaff: because
within the very essence of the national temperament exists not
only a sense of humour but a closely allied and deeply satiric sense
of the futility of military ambition, as an end in itself: ' There's
honour for you '. The more continental and Fascist Hotspur,
like Tybalt in *Romeo and Juliet*—we may remember the very
English Mercutio's caustic criticisms of Tybalt's explicitly continental swaggerings—seems trivial by comparison; though of
course Hal must eventually prove himself the better soldier.
This, too, has before now happened with Great Britain, as a
nation.

When Hal succeeds to the throne his brothers and the Chief
Justice, who had once imprisoned him when Prince of Wales, are
at first fearful, but the new king disabuses them in a phrase holding
the very soul of British sovereignty, national or imperial, in
opposition to a Tamburlaine's or Hitler's tyranny:

> Brothers, you mix your sadness with some fear ;
> This is the English, not the Turkish court ;
> Not Amurath an Amurath succeeds
> But Harry Harry.
> (*2 Henry IV*, V. ii. 46.)

A quotation for that most testing moment, the moment of triumph,
whether personal, official, or national. So, too, when the Chief
Justice, whom the new king addresses first with some severity,
offers a noble defence in terms of justice, he is answered by a
speech of youthful humility, unlike the voice of any previous
king; for this king is to be different from all predecessors, at once
humble, religious, and assured in action.

Richard III is terrifyingly powerful—but wicked. Richard II
is weak, but, under disaster, becomes almost a saint, religious
phraseology so appropriately accompanying practical failure that

a want in our religious tradition is suggested. The troubled Henry IV is really neither one thing nor the other, neither a first-class villain nor a beautiful failure. Now in Henry V Shakespeare attempts a blend of righteousness with power.

To fuse strong action with religious humility is, however, far from easy. In Marlowe's *Tamburlaine* we have an amazing tale of conquest, the hero starting as a peasant, conquering nation after nation in scene after scene, and ending as all but master of the world. His aspiring pride rises in rhetoric of ringing, resounding, clanging magnificence. City after city falls before him. The tone is pagan, barbaric, and often brutal. Tamburlaine makes cruel mockery of his enemies, subjugating them to his power-lust, his pagan splendour being, precisely, a denial of chivalry. Through all he feels himself irresistible, backed by destiny, at once the overthrower of religions and himself ' the scourge of God '. Here we have Hitler's very progress viewed more as a German sympathiser might view it, with all its superficial glamour, but none of those inward depths of psychic conflict shadowed by Shakespeare in *Richard III*. In *Henry V* Shakespeare—who clearly parodies such bombast through the absurd braggadocio and misquoted Marlovian tags of Pistol—writes his *Tamburlaine*: and it is vastly different from Marlowe's.

Shakespeare's hero has already been contrasted with an Amurath, and is now to become a Christian warrior, leading, after long periods of civil war, a united nation to foreign conquest. The various strands of religion, royalty, and humour, separated out and frayed in *Henry IV*, are to be close knotted in the person of Henry V; though Falstaff has been necessarily rejected, with a sharp repudiation of his irresistible wit—' Reply not to me with a fool-born jest ' (*2 Henry IV*, V. v. 60)—that strikes at that dangerous tendency in the Anglo-Saxon temperament to shirk responsibilities by an easy humour. The stage is now left free for a new epic and heroic drama, blending Christian virtue with martial prowess. The largeness of his theme, more epic than dramatic, embarrassed even Shakespeare, leading him to preface the separate acts of *Henry V* with a sequence of fine choruses. Here is the first:

> O for a Muse of fire, that would ascend
> The brightest heaven of invention,

A kingdom for a stage, princes to act
And monarchs to behold the swelling scene !
Then should the warlike Harry, like himself,
Assume the port of Mars ; and at his heels,
Leash'd in like hounds, should famine, sword, and fire
Crouch for employment.   But pardon, gentles all,
The flat unraised spirits that hath dared
On this unworthy scaffold to bring forth
So great an object : can this cockpit hold
The vasty fields of France ? or may we cram
Within this wooden O the very casques
That did affright the air at Agincourt ?
O, pardon ! since a crooked figure may
Attest in little place a million ;
And let us, ciphers to this great accompt,
On your imaginary forces work.
Suppose within the girdle of these walls
Are now confined two mighty monarchies,
Whose high upreared and abutting fronts
The perilous narrow ocean parts asunder :
Piece out our imperfections with your thoughts ;
Into a thousand parts divide one man,
And make imaginary puissance ;
Think, when we talk of horses, that you see them
Printing their proud hoofs i' the receiving earth ;
For 'tis your thoughts that now must deck our kings,
Carry them here and there ; jumping o'er times,
Turning the accomplishment of many years
Into an hour-glass : for the which supply,
Admit me Chorus to this history ;
Who prologue-like your humble patience pray,
Gently to hear, kindly to judge, our play.

                                                            (I. i. 1.)

Twice only throughout his work Shakespeare apologises for the
insufficiency of his art: here, and in the prologue to *Henry VIII.*
'Famine, sword, and fire': war is not sentimentalised.   Though
Shakespeare attempts to Christianise military conquest, he never
lets us forget that it is military conquest, with its attendant terrors,
that he is Christianising.   Nor is the Falstaffian approach ever
quite forgotten: though their massive progenitor be dead, Pistol,
Bardolph, and Nym carry on, and are supported by that glorious
comic triumvirate, the officers, Jamy the Scot, Macmorris the
Irishman and, best of all, Fluellen, the Welshman, chattering of
Monmouth, military science, and the 'wars of Alexander'.

King Henry is a deeply religious man, phrase after phrase showing his reliance on God. He will not fight until his claims on France are sanctioned, in terms of 'law' and 'right', by the Archbishop of Canterbury, to whose legal scholarship he appeals, with a stern warning that no prevarication be allowed to twist the truth in a matter so likely to involve grievous sufferings: never does he forget those.

The King is to lead a united nation to war. Shakespeare's mood is therefore ripe for some fine comments on national harmony:

> For government, though high and low and lower,
> Put into parts, doth keep in one consent,
> Congreeing in a full and natural close,
> Like music.

(I. ii. 180.)

The uncannily precise social ordering of the life of bees, the ' singing masons building roofs of gold ', is introduced as an analogy, wherein different tasks are appointed to different individuals, with the following conclusion:

> I this infer,
> That many things, having full reference
> To one consent, may work contrariously :
> As many arrows, loosed several ways,
> Fly to one mark ; as many ways meet in one town ;
> As many fresh streams meet in one salt sea ;
> As many lines close in the dial's centre ;
> So may a thousand actions, once afoot,
> End in one purpose, and be all well borne
> Without defeat.

(I. ii. 204.)

So King Henry, with a unified nation at his back, may safely set out for France.

The messenger from the Dauphin is called in, and shows himself afraid to deliver his master's message. The King's comment is important:

> We are no tyrant, but a Christian king ;
> Under whose grace our passion is as subject
> As are our wretches fetter'd in our prisons. . . .

(I. ii. 241.)

You can see how carefully Shakespeare is labouring to create in

Henry a blend of Christian faith and martial heroism.   How uncannily, too, the King typifies the English temperament when, discovering that the Dauphin's message is merely a gift of tennis-balls, as a taunt against his own supposed decadence, he answers:

> We are glad the Dauphin is so pleasant with us:
> His present and your pains we thank you for:
> When we have match'd our rackets to these balls,
> We will, in France, by God's grace, play a set
> Shall strike his father's crown into the hazard.
> Tell him he hath made a match with such a wrangler
> That all the courts of France will be disturb'd
> With chaces.   And we understand him well,
> How he comes o'er us with our wilder days,
> Not measuring what use we made of them.
> We never valued this poor seat of England;
> And therefore, living hence, did give ourself
> To barbarous licence; as 'tis ever common
> That men are merriest when they are from home.
> But tell the Dauphin I will keep my state,
> Be like a king and show my sail of greatness
> When I do rouse me in my throne of France:
> For that I have laid by my majesty,
> And plodded like a man for working-days;
> But I will rise there with so full a glory
> That I will dazzle all the eyes of France,
> Yea, strike the Dauphin blind to look on us.
> And tell the pleasant prince this mock of his
> Hath turn'd his balls to gun-stones; and his soul
> Shall stand sore charged for the wasteful vengeance
> That shall fly with them: for many a thousand widows
> Shall this his mock mock out of their dear husbands;
> Mock mothers from their sons, mock castles down;
> And some are yet ungotten and unborn
> That shall have cause to curse the Dauphin's scorn.
> But this lies all within the will of God,
> To whom I do appeal; and in whose name
> Tell you the Dauphin I am coming on,
> To venge me as I may and to put forth
> My rightful hand in a well-hallow'd cause.
> So get you hence in peace; and tell the Dauphin
> His jest will savour but of shallow wit,
> When thousands weep more than did laugh at it.
>   (I. ii. 259.)

It happened with Hotspur before; it has happened often since.

It happens in our time. 'We never valued our poor seat of England': we did not. And yet Drake is never more dangerous than when at his bowls on Plymouth Hoe.

Before embarking, the King discovers treachery in three nobles, suborned by foreign money, and commits the culprits to their doom, with a speech of scorching rhetoric on deception and ingratitude—that *bête noire* of the Shakespearian universe—which gains poignancy from our own experience, and fears, of treachery. In France he wins a swift victory at Harfleur, preluded by the famous 'Once more unto the breach, dear friends', urging his men to put by the 'modest stillness and humility' so valued in peace, and instead now to 'disguise fair nature with hard-favour'd rage' and 'imitate the action of the tiger' (III. i. 1): an embarrassing counsel which our own pacific tendencies must face. Henry V is himself once, in the much earlier play, *1 Henry VI* (I. i. 8–16), compared to an especially dazzling, sun-brilliant, and therefore royal, dragon. Animal strength holds various meanings drawn from both sides of the Saint George symbolism: the horses and greyhounds so vivid in *Henry V* are fine beasts, corresponding to a strength which is virtue:

> On, on, you noblest English,
> Whose blood is fet from fathers of war-proof!
> Fathers that, like so many Alexanders,
> Have in these parts from morn till even fought,
> And sheathed their swords for lack of argument.
> Dishonour not your mothers; now attest
> That those whom you call'd fathers did beget you.
> Be copy now to men of grosser blood,
> And teach them how to war. And you, good yeomen,
> Whose limbs were made in England, show us here
> The mettle of your pasture; let us swear
> That you are worth your breeding; which I doubt not;
> For there is none of you so mean and base,
> That hath not noble lustre in your eyes.
> I see you stand like greyhounds in the slips,
> Straining upon the start. The game's afoot:
> Follow your spirit, and upon this charge
> Cry 'God for Harry, England and Saint George!'
>
> (III. i. 17)

The King had been sportive in his youth; and now war is conceived as a 'game', though without mitigation of its terror. Later

Henry implores the citizens of Harfleur to surrender, warning them of the horrors that await them if once the instincts of his soldiery be unleashed:

> Therefore, you men of Harfleur,
> Take pity of your town and of your people,
> Whiles yet my soldiers are in my command;
> Whiles yet the cool and temperate wind of grace
> O'erblows the filthy and contagious clouds
> Of heady murder, spoil, and villainy.
>
> (III. iii. 27.)

It is a long speech. No more honest facing of war's brutality was ever penned.

But, as though to show us that such direct heroism is not, by itself, enough, we advance to the far more crucial battle of Agincourt. The English, as a fine chorus describes them, are now battle-worn and exhausted, and surrounded by a more powerful, and fresh, army. Only a miracle can save them. The King, disguising his anxiety, goes through his army cheering his men, like a 'sun', calling them 'brothers' (Chorus to Act IV); and later, putting on a disguise, hears the not unreasonable complaint of a common soldier, who knows nothing of the issues at stake, and, when told that the King's cause is just, answers, pithily, 'That's more than we know' (IV. i. 136). The soldier's arguments are incisive. Left alone, the King meditates upon the intolerable burden laid on him:

> Upon the king! let us our lives, our souls,
> Our debts, our careful wives,
> Our children and our sins lay on the king!
> We must bear all. O hard condition,
> Twin-born with greatness, subject to the breath
> Of every fool, whose sense no more can feel
> But his own wringing! What infinite heart's-ease
> Must kings neglect, that private men enjoy!
>
> (IV. i. 250.)

What joy does power give to compensate for this heavy, spiritual, weight? 'Ceremony', that is all, the tinsel trappings of material magnificence:

> And what art thou, thou idol ceremony?
>
> (IV. i. 260.)

What a difference from *Tamburlaine*! Temporal power has its reverse side: a thought one might extend to the apparent riches and yet heavy responsibilities of imperial control. So ' ceremony ' is impugned, as an outward deceit:

> Canst thou, when thou command'st the beggar's knee,
> Command the health of it ? No, thou proud dream,
> That play'st so subtly with a king's repose;
> I am a king that find thee, and I know
> 'Tis not the balm, the sceptre and the ball,
> The sword, the mace, the crown imperial,
> The intertissued robe of gold and pearl,
> The farced title running 'fore the king,
> The throne he sits on, nor the tide of pomp
> That beats upon the high shore of this world,
> No, not all these, thrice-gorgeous ceremony,
> Not all these, laid in bed majestical,
> Can sleep so soundly as the wretched slave,
> Who with a body fill'd and vacant mind
> Gets him to rest, cramm'd with distressful bread;
> Never sees horrid night, the child of hell,
> But, like a lackey, from the rise to set
> Sweats in the eye of Phoebus and all night
> Sleeps in Elysium.
>
> (IV. i. 276.)

Yet, too, what deep burnishings of poetry Shakespeare accords those regal splendours. Indeed, it is precisely because he sees through them, knows their purely provisional value, that all Shakespeare's kingly impressions hold such lasting potency. They are always sinking into depths beyond our understanding, are fed from elsewhere; they are sacramental.

Next Henry throws himself and his army on God's mercy, confessing his father's crime against the sacred person of Richard; that is, confessing, as perhaps all temporal leaders must, the dubious nature of his own authority, bought and maintained in blood:

> O God of battles ! steel my soldiers' hearts;
> Possess them not with fear; take from them now
> The sense of reckoning, if the opposed numbers
> Pluck their hearts from them. Not to-day, O Lord,
> O, not to-day, think not upon the fault
> My father made in compassing the crown !
> I Richard's body have interr'd anew;
> And on it have bestow'd more contrite tears

Than from it issued forced drops of blood :
Five hundred poor I have in yearly pay,
Who twice a day their wither'd hands hold up
Toward heaven, to pardon blood ; and I have built
Two chantries, where the sad and solemn priests
Sing still for Richard's soul.   More will I do ;
Though all that I can do is nothing worth,
Since that my penitence comes after all,
Imploring pardon.

(IV. i. 309.)

The ghost of Richard has, through repeated reminders, and
especially in the old king's confession to his son, lingered as an
accusing presence throughout *Henry IV* : but now that ghost is
laid.   From now on Henry is free ; and when one of his nobles
wishes for more men, accuses such fear with the finest heroic
assurance in our literature.   Reading, let the passage start collo-
quially, only gradually awaking to its full blaze, and watch for a
subtle touch of humour :

What's he that wishes so ?
My cousin Westmoreland ?   No, my fair cousin :
If we are mark'd to die, we are enow
To do our country loss ; and if to live,
The fewer men, the greater share of honour.
God's will !   I pray thee, wish not one man more.
By Jove, I am not covetous for gold,
Nor care I who doth feed upon my cost ;
It yearns me not if men my garments wear ;
Such outward things dwell not in my desires :
But if it be a sin to covet honour,
I am the most offending soul alive.
No, faith, my coz, wish not a man from England :
God's peace !   I would not lose so great an honour
As one man more, methinks, would share from me
For the best hope I have.   O, do not wish one more !
Rather proclaim it, Westmoreland, through my host,
That he which hath no stomach to this fight,
Let him depart ; his passport shall be made
And crowns for convoy put into his purse.
We would not die in that man's company
That fears his fellowship to die with us.
This day is call'd the feast of Crispian :
He that outlives this day, and comes safe home,
Will stand a tip-toe when this day is named,
And rouse him at the name of Crispian.

He that shall live this day, and see old age,
Will yearly on the vigil feast his neighbours,
And say, ' To-morrow is Saint Crispian '.
Then will he strip his sleeve and show his scars,
And say ' These wounds I had on Crispin's day '.
Old men forget ; yet all shall be forgot,
But he'll remember with advantages
What feats he did that day : then shall our names,
Familiar in his mouth as household words,
Harry the king, Bedford and Exeter,
Warwick and Talbot, Salisbury and Gloucester
Be in their flowing cups freshly remember'd.
This story shall the good man teach his son ;
And Crispin Crispian shall ne'er go by,
From this day to the ending of the world,
But we in it shall be remembered ;
We few, we happy few, we band of brothers ;
For he to-day that sheds his blood with me
Shall be my brother ; be he ne'er so vile,
This day shall gentle his condition :
And gentlemen in England now a-bed
Shall think themselves accursed they were not here,
And hold their manhoods cheap whiles any speaks
That fought with us upon Saint Crispin's day.

(IV. iii. 18.)

Many other fights where material weakness has contested against heavy odds have been more important to the world's history than Agincourt; many heroisms are more gripping to the imagination— Spartans at Thermopylae, Drake's seamen against the Armada, our own airmen to-day; but none were ever so phrased and, indeed, all find here their own consummate expression. Earlier King Henry called on God and Saint George, and now we have Saint Crispin, a name whose very sound delicately suggests Christ; and yet how careful Shakespeare is to avoid directly associating Christ Himself with any martial assertion, however chivalrous. It has been observed that Shakespeare's Henry becomes here a comrade of his own men. But there is no levelling down of the King to his subjects, not a hair's breadth of his status is renounced. No. But his soldiers, through heroism, are lifted up to the stature of his own sovereignty; and in this very distinction lies the difference between what is most sacred and what most pernicious in socialist doctrine. Notice, too, how this speech gains power from raising its hearers' own, deeper, selves: it appeals to their own judgments, asking them to be true to themselves, as in the earlier 'follow your spirits' or

> nought shall make us rue
> If England to itself do rest but true.

(King John, V. vii. 117.)

Such 'truth' is the key to much in Shakespeare.

When the battle of Agincourt is won, the King attributes the glory of it to God:

King Henry :   O God, thy arm was here;
And not to us, but to thy arm alone,
Ascribe we all ! When, without stratagem,
But in plain shock and even play of battle,
Was ever known so great and little loss
On one part and on th'other ? Take it, God,
For it is none but thine !

Exeter :   'Tis wonderful !

King Henry : Come, go we in procession to the village :
And be it death proclaimed through our host
To boast of this or take the praise from God
Which is his only.

Fluellen : Is't not lawful, an't please your majesty, to tell how many
is killed ?

King Henry : Yes, captain; but with this acknowledgement, that God
fought for us.

Fluellen : Yes, my conscience, he did us great good.

King Henry : Do we all holy rites;
Let there be sung ' Non nobis ' and ' Te Deum ';
The dead with charity enclosed in clay :
We'll then to Calais; and to England then;
Where ne'er from France arrived more happy men.

(IV. viii. 111.)

In *Henry* Shakespeare characterises a model of English generalship. The King's humility is contrasted with continental boasting; and during the battle of Agincourt criticism is levelled (by Fluellen) against the enemy's methods. A short passage sums up, in a more realistic manner, the kind of virtue intended:

> We would have all such offenders so cut off : and we give express charge that in our marches through the country there be nothing compelled from the villages, nothing taken but paid for, none of the French upbraided or abused in disdainful language; for when lenity

and cruelty play for a kingdom, the gentler gamester is the soonest winner.

(III. vi. 116.)

With that we may close our study of Henry's warring.

The play ends in concord.   Peace is eulogised by the Duke of Burgundy and Henry woos Katherine of France.   Here is Burgundy's speech, spoken before the two kings:

> Let it not disgrace me
> If I demand before this royal view,
> What rub or what impediment there is,
> Why that the naked, poor, and mangled Peace,
> Dear nurse of arts, plenties, and joyful births,
> Should not in this best garden of the world,
> Our fertile France, put up her lovely visage?
> Alas! she hath from France too long been chas'd,
> And all her husbandry doth lie on heaps,
> Corrupting in its own fertility.
> Her vine, the merry cheerer of the heart,
> Unpruned dies; her hedges even-pleach'd,
> Like prisoners wildly overgrown with hair,
> Put forth disorder'd twigs; her fallow leas
> The darnel, hemlock and rank fumitory
> Doth root upon, while that the coulter rusts
> That should deracinate such savagery;
> The even mead, that erst brought sweetly forth
> The freckled cowslip, burnet, and green clover,
> Wanting the scythe, all uncorrected, rank,
> Conceives by idleness, and nothing teems
> But hateful docks, rough thistles, kecksies, burs,
> Losing both beauty and utility;
> And as our vineyards, fallows, meads, and hedges,
> Defective in their natures, grow to wildness,
> Even so our houses and ourselves and children
> Have lost, or do not learn for want of time,
> The sciences that should become our country,
> But grow like savages—as soldiers will,
> That nothing do but meditate on blood—
> To swearing and stern looks, diffus'd attire,
> And everything that seems unnatural.
> Which to reduce into our former favour
> You are assembled; and my speech entreats
> That I may know the let why gentle Peace
> Should not expel these inconveniences,
> And bless us with her former qualities.

(V. ii. 31.)

We may remember Henry VI's longing for nature's simple sweets. Burgundy's pastoral lines crown, as with a chaplet of flowers, Shakespeare's historic sequence.

This sequence, together with the comedies (whose resolving action—always, in its way, a definition of essential peace—is usually played out across a background of war and civil disturbance), makes up the first half of Shakespeare's work. The second half is a repetition of the first, with a similar conclusion.

IV

CRACK OF DOOM

IN the plays so far noticed the conflict of human purpose and the will of God has not been finally resolved. *Henry V* is a magnificent attempt, but there are questions left over. Henry's warring is not all merciful: it could not be. Duke Theseus in *A Midsummer Night's Dream* personifies the desired union. He is gracious and kindly, though a great conqueror; but we do not actually see him at anything more bloodthirsty than hunting, and even then he seems mainly interested in the music of his hounds' baying, very much being subtly kept in the background. The Elizabethan age continually aspired to the synthesis of sweet gentleness and soldierly prowess, of which Sir Philip Sidney was a famed example; which breathes in Lyly's *Alexander and Campaspe*; which Spenser's *Faerie Queene* is working to define and inculcate; which Shakespeare suggests in those lines attributing to Hamlet ' the courtier's, scholar's, soldier's, eye, tongue, sword '.

The second half of Shakespeare's work does not repudiate the sequence leading to *Henry V*, but treats the old materials with a more deeply critical handling. Nurse Cavell's famous ' Patriotism is not enough ' might well be taken as a text for this new movement. It is as though Falstaff came back to life to inspire not comedy but tragedy. Falstaff becomes, as it were, violent; the mountain of a man turns out to be a volcano; there is earthquake and tempest, and seas grow tumultuous. This turbulence the ship of Shakespeare's national faith has to weather—and what a storm it is to be, upheaving waters and showing the slimy ocean bed, whirling you to the stars, dragging you out of your course. A veritable tornado is endured before that ship, in *Henry VIII*, comes to harbour.

The greater plays we are to notice make, of course, statements far outspacing any national assertion. Those statements I have analysed in former studies. My comments here will be brief, and strictly limited to my present purpose.

Both *Julius Caesar* and *Hamlet* form a valuable contrast to *Henry V*, showing heroes deeply troubled by the necessity of stern action involving bloodshed.   Honour demands that Brutus assassinate his friend Caesar in the cause of political liberty, but, whereas Cassius on the one side and Antony on the other are forceful and single-minded, Brutus, though acting for so pure an ideal as 'liberty', endures a conflict leading to disaster:

> Between the acting of a dreadful thing
> And the first motion, all the interim is
> Like a phantasma or a hideous dream.
> The genius and the mortal instruments
> Are then in council; and the state of man,
> Like to a little kingdom, suffers then
> The nature of an insurrection.
>
> (II. i. 63.)

That is the new and deeper note.

In *Hamlet* we are shown a hero of sensitive temperament, who learns from a Ghost that his father's untimely end has been caused by the treacherous act of his own uncle, now king.   Hamlet's world is henceforth darkened, and society, to him, diseased. Honour demands that he execute revenge, but his will is paralysed. He typifies all great men whose depth of insight prevents them from obeying the calls of action in a disordered world.   He is, moreover, contrasted with Laertes and Fortinbras, strong young men serving ideals of conventional honour without a questioning thought.   ' Am I a coward ? ' Hamlet asks himself, wondering if he is a greater or a lesser than those around him.   His two longest soliloquies, those beginning ' O what a rogue and peasant slave am I!' (II. ii. 584) and ' How all occasions do inform against me . . .' (IV. iv. 32), are indicative; and both may serve to reflect the soul of England during the last twenty years, suffering inward division and tortured by depth of insight and maturity of experience leading to what appears a relaxation of militancy, while younger, and seemingly more virile, nations, Italy and Germany, get down to business with the thoughtless energies of a Laertes or a Fortinbras.   The play's action is given a war-like setting and these two soliloquies are occasioned directly by thoughts of war, its horrors and heroisms; the one by the Player's speech on the sack of Troy, the other by Fortinbras' expedition against the Poles:

> Now, whe'r it be
> Bestial oblivion, or some craven scruple
> Of thinking too precisely on the event,

A thought, which, quarter'd, hath but one part wisdom,
And ever three parts coward, I do not know
Why yet I live to say ' This thing's to do ';
Sith I have cause and will and strength and means
To do't.   Examples gross as earth exhort me :
Witness this army of such mass and charge
Led by a delicate and tender prince,
Whose spirit with divine ambition puff'd
Makes mouths at the invisible event,
Exposing what is mortal and unsure
To all that fortune, death, and danger dare,
Even for an egg-shell.   Rightly to be great
Is not to stir without great argument,
But greatly to find quarrel in a straw
When honour's at the stake.   How stand I then,
That have a father kill'd, a mother stain'd,
Excitements of my reason and my blood,
And let all sleep, while, to my shame, I see
The imminent death of twenty thousand men,
That, for a fantasy and trick of fame,
Go to their graves like beds, fight for a plot
Whereon the numbers cannot try the cause,
Which is not tomb enough and continent
To hide the slain ?   O ! from this time forth,
My thoughts be bloody, or be nothing worth !

(IV. iv. 39.)

' Bloody ' here means ' virile ' rather than ' murderous ', as so often in Shakespeare.

But Hamlet's lack of virility is clearly one with his profundity, and Shakespeare's greater plays to follow all preserve something of the Hamlet spirit: the poet is not content with military or national values alone, but remains deeply concerned with them, and henceforth submits each and all to a penetrating criticism, showing them in contrast, or collaboration, with greater, and mysterious, presences.   Shakespeare is himself now ghost-ridden and, like Hamlet, aims to penetrate below the surface of an unclean society by his own dramatic art: ' The play's the thing . . .'   So too, by the reverse process, we may ourselves search for solutions to our own national problems in the mirror of our national drama.

All international problems are closely related to home government; and, as I have argued, no final distinction can be drawn between military and civil force. The order upheld by the King in *Hamlet* is both reasonably efficient and humane, yet based on crime: that is the paradox which renders the play so baffling. Elsewhere this subtlest of difficulties is more directly attacked. What has Shakespeare to say of government? His thought is, as usual, characterised by a unique balancing of opposites, here justice and Christian mercy. Remember Portia's speech in the *Merchant of Venice*:

> The quality of mercy is not strain'd,
> It droppeth as the gentle rain from heaven
> Upon the place beneath : it is twice bless'd ;
> It blesseth him that gives and him that takes :
> 'Tis mightiest in the mightiest ; it becomes
> The throned monarch better than his crown.
> His sceptre shows the force of temporal power,
> The attribute to awe and majesty,
> Wherein doth sit the dread and fear of kings ;
> But mercy is above this sceptred sway,
> It is enthroned in the hearts of kings,
> It is an attribute to God himself,
> And earthly power doth then show likest God's
> When mercy seasons justice. Therefore, Jew,
> Though justice be thy plea, consider this,
> That in the course of justice none of us
> Should see salvation : we do pray for mercy,
> And that same prayer doth teach us all to render
> The deeds of mercy. I have spoke thus much
> To mitigate the justice of thy plea,
> Which if thou follow, this strict court of Venice
> Must needs give sentence 'gainst the merchant there.
>
> (IV. i. 184.)

The transcending of harsh law is, as it must be, felt as one with royalty. A king is far more than a governor: he is rather a mediator between the temporal and the eternal.

In *Measure for Measure* Shakespeare closely advances his analysis of a deeply disturbing problem. Is justice possible? The studious Duke of Vienna, whose psychological insight has convinced him so thoroughly of man's inability to pronounce judgment on his neighbour that his city becomes a riot of vice, hands over ducal authority to a man of stern rectitude and spotless reputation, and next returns, in disguise, to watch the result.

Angelo, the substitute, is shown as failing under the test of authority and himself, at a key moment, guilty of the very fault he would punish. The whole play turns, as I have shown at length in *The Wheel of Fire*, on the serene but baffling teaching of Christ's gospel. Great things are spoken. Here is one:

> Well, believe this,
> No ceremony that to great ones 'longs,
> Not the king's crown, nor the deputed sword,
> The marshal's truncheon, nor the judge's robe,
> Become them with one half so good a grace
> As mercy does.
>
> (II. ii. 58.)

And here another:

> Why, all the souls that were were forfeit once;
> And He that might the vantage best have took,
> Found out the remedy. How would you be,
> If He, which is the top of judgment, should
> But judge you as you are? O! think on that,
> And mercy then will breathe within your lips,
> Like man new made.
>
> (II. ii. 73.)

And this perhaps the best of all:

> O! it is excellent
> To have a giant's strength, but it is tyrannous
> To use it like a giant. . . . Could great men thunder
> As Jove himself does, Jove would ne'er be quiet,
> For every pelting, petty officer
> Would use his heaven for thunder; nothing but thunder.
> Merciful heaven!
> Thou rather with thy sharp and sulphurous bolt
> Split'st the unwedgeable and gnarled oak
> Than the soft myrtle; but man, proud man,
> Drest in a little brief authority,
> Most ignorant of what he's most assur'd,
> His glassy essence, like an angry ape,
> Plays such fantastic tricks before high heaven
> As make the angels weep; who, with our spleens,
> Would all themselves laugh mortal.
>
> (II. ii. 107.)

In this day of iron disciplines and state-officials lording it over their betters, we do well to remember that such things are no new and clever inventions but an age-old tendency of government on which Shakespeare has pronounced such judgments as these in the name of Christ, who himself uttered all but the last word on such oppositions: ' You could have no power over me were it not given you from above '. And yet Shakespeare leaves us in no doubt that Vienna needed a strong ruler. The problem seems insoluble.

Temporal authority must, as things are, exist. In *Troilus and Cressida* Agamemnon is too ready to fall back on semi-mystic excuses of tragic philosophy—in which he bears some resemblance to the Duke in *Measure for Measure*—for his, and his army's, failure. He is answered by Ulysses with a long speech on order.* Ulysses' lines may assist our diagnosis of the western world's recent lack of unity by pointing us to those parents of all unity, reverence and respect:

> The specialty of rule hath been neglected :
> And look, how many Grecian tents do stand
> Hollow upon this plain, so many hollow factions.
> When that the general is not like the hive
> To whom the foragers shall all repair,
> What honey is expected ?   Degree being vizarded,
> The unworthiest shows as fairly in the mask.
> The heavens themselves, the planets, and this centre
> Observe degree, priority, and place,
> Insisture, course, proportion, season, form,
> Office, and custom, in all line of order :
> And therefore is the glorious planet Sol
> In noble eminence enthron'd and spher'd
> Amidst the other ; whose med'cinable eye
> Corrects the ill aspects of planets evil,
> And posts, like the commandment of a king,
> Sans check, to good and bad : but when the planets
> In evil mixture to disorder wander,
> What plagues, and what portents, what mutiny,
> What raging of the sea, shaking of earth,
> Commotion in the winds, frights, changes, horrors,
> Divert and crack, rend and deracinate
> The unity and married calm of states
> Quite from their fixure !   O ! when degree is shak'd,
> Which is the ladder to all high designs,

---

* Cp. the opposition of Falstaff and the Chief Justice in *2 Henry IV* as analysed by Prof. Dover Wilson in *The Fortunes of Falstaff* (Falstaff corresponding to the tragic spirit of later plays).

The enterprise is sick.   How could communities,
Degrees in schools, and brotherhoods in cities,
Peaceful commerce from dividable shores,
The primogenitive and due of birth,
Prerogative of age, crowns, sceptres, laurels,
But by degree, stand in authentic place ?
Take but degree away, untune that string,
And, hark ! what discord follows ; each thing meets
In mere oppugnancy : the bounded waters
Should lift their bosoms higher than the shores,
And make a sop of all this solid globe :
Strength should be lord of imbecility,
And the rude son should strike his father dead :
Force should be right ; or rather, right and wrong—
Between whose endless jar justice resides—
Should lose their names, and so should justice too.
Then every thing includes itself in power,
Power into will, will into appetite ;
And appetite, a universal wolf,
So doubly seconded with will and power,
Must make perforce a universal prey,
And last eat up himself.   Great Agamemnon,
This chaos, when degree is suffocate,
Follows the choking.
And this neglection of degree it is
That by a pace goes backward, with a purpose
It hath to climb.   The general's disdain'd
By him one step below, he by the next,
That next by him beneath ; so every step,
Exampled by the first pace that is sick
Of his superior, grows to an envious fever
Of pale and bloodless emulation :
And 'tis this fever that keeps Troy on foot,
Not her own sinews.   To end a tale of length,
Troy in our weakness lives, not in her strength.

                                        (I. iii. 78.)

That slow working out of a stable system from chaos and conflict
dramatised in the historical plays is here given its philosophy; and
that philosophy is one which presses on us heavily with a summon-
ing insistence, not merely as nations, but as travaillers towards that
world-order of which our present war is the birth-pangs.   Notice
how all Christian, and other civilised, values are by Shakespeare
maintained; values which Germany in her masterful will to a
forced, inorganic, order scatters to the four winds.

In *Troilus and Cressida* both government and war, as well as love, the play's primary theme, are variously honoured and satirised. On the Trojan side war is chivalrous and romantic, with honour an infinite value, but among the Greeks it is shown as brutal and all but absurd. The deformed and embittered Thersites watches two lords fighting during a battle, and cheers them on with bitter mockery. Elsewhere he comments:

> Lechery, lechery; still, wars and lechery: nothing else holds fashion. A burning devil take them!
>
> (V. iii. 192.)

Remembering Falstaff we can feel Shakespeare wondering whether all armed conflict is finally stupid and degrading, and the history of modern Europe, as Swift saw it, poisoned at the source of national action. Such bitterness is expanded further in *Timon of Athens*.

Here Shakespeare sets his soul on paper as perhaps in no other work, not even *Hamlet*. We are shown a generous and lordly Athenian who exhausts his wealth and, all help from his former friends being denied him, is struck to the quick by their miserly ingratitude; next deserts humanity for a hermit's garb and sea-shore cavern home, only to find more gold when digging for roots; but, the iron having settled in his heart, refuses now all compromise, pours out his new-found treasure to assist Alcibiades to lead an army against Athens, and indeed gives gold, with imprecations, to all who come; but himself will not return, though the repentant city implores him to lend his name and princely virtue to save them from destruction. We must be ready to put London for Athens as we read Timon's prophetic denunciations. He shatters the smug surfaces of our civilisation with a piercing invective, exposing its sores and shames and hideous communal wrongs:

> I know thee too; and more than that I know thee
> I not desire to know. Follow thy drum;
> With man's blood paint the ground, gules, gules;
> Religious canons, civil laws are cruel;
> Then what should war be?
>
> (IV. iii. 57.)

' Drum ' is spoken with emphasised scorn of war's childish ritual;

while the charge against civil ordinances is levelled in terms of cruelty. Hearing Alcibiades is campaigning against Athens, Timon next gives him gold, and in part seriously and partly in scathing irony—for detestation of war breathes in every pitying yet condemning syllable—directs him to violent excesses:

Timon : Warr'st thou 'gainst Athens?
Alcibiades : Ay, Timon, and have cause.
Timon : The gods confound them all in thy conquest;
And thee after, when thou hast conquer'd!
Alcibiades : Why me, Timon?
Timon : That, by killing of villains, thou wast born to conquer my country.
Put up thy gold: go on—here's gold—go on;
Be as a planetary plague, when Jove
Will o'er some high-vic'd city hang his poison
In the sick air: let not thy sword skip one.
Pity not honour'd age for his white beard;
He is a usurer. Strike me the counterfeit matron;
It is her habit only that is honest,
Herself's a bawd. Let not the virgin's cheek
Make soft thy trenchant sword; for those milk-paps,
That through the window-bars bore at men's eyes,
Are not within the leaf of pity writ,
But set them down horrible traitors. Spare not the babe,
Whose dimpled smiles from fools exhaust their mercy;
Think it a bastard, whom the oracle
Hath doubtfully pronounc'd thy throat shall cut,
And mince it sans remorse. Swear against objects;
Put armour on thine ears and on thine eyes,
Whose proof nor yells of mothers, maids, nor babes,
Nor sight of priests in holy vestments bleeding,
Shall pierce a jot. There's gold to pay thy soldiers:
Make large confusion; and, thy fury spent,
Confounded be thyself! Speak not, be gone.
(IV. iii. 102.)

What has become of the romantic Henry V? Yet even there you will find, in Henry's own speeches, a closely similar awareness of war's brutality. Here words such as ' my country ', the various images of human appeal, the ' holy priests ' and ' sacred vestments ', all witness, are stamped with a recognition of, those potential excellences that have been betrayed by a decadent society. In another speech Timon's words labour under an agonised sense of

war's hideousness even when his refusal to assist the senate rings
final:

> Well, sir, I will; therefore, I will, sir; thus :—
> If Alcibiades kill my countrymen,
> Let Alcibiades know this of Timon,
> That Timon cares not.   But if he sack fair Athens,
> And take our goodly aged men by the beards,
> Giving our holy virgins to the stain
> Of contumelious, beastly, mad-brain'd war;
> Then let him know, and tell him Timon speaks it,
> In pity of our aged and our youth,
> I cannot choose but tell him, that I care not,
> And let him take't at worst.

(V. i. 173.)

It may seem, indeed, that Shakespeare prefers Alcibiades, the man
of soldierly honour, to the usurous and capitalistic senators.   But
Timon himself despises both and all their ways and works:

> Be Alcibiades your plague, you his,
> And last so long enough.

(V. i. 194.)

Timon is on a height overlooking all military, or civil, ambitions.

The play does, however, forecast our present great conflict to the
extent that it correctly diagnoses the forces at issue, the emerging
opposition of (i) a peace-loving capitalism, rendered ugly in its
'dotage' by 'usury' (III. v. 101) in high places, resting in
'great chairs of ease' (V. iv. 11) and relying, as do the Senators
in their scene with Alcibiades, on smug concepts of law and
justice, and (ii) stark, youthful, militarism in revolt.   Alcibiades
certainly wins and establishes a new order.   I read the play as a
terrible warning to Great Britain; as an extension of old John
Gaunt's denunciation of an England bound in 'by inky blots and
rotten parchment bonds' in *Richard II*.   If any doubts remain
that Shakespeare's genius here senses the oncoming of vast, greed-
engendered, conflicts, they should be dispelled by Timon's address
(IV. iii. 25–44) to the gold-nugget he digs up, called by him a
'yellow slave' that can 'knit and break religions' and bend all
mankind to its will, putting 'odds' (i.e. conflict) 'among the rout
of nations':

> O thou sweet king-killer, and dear divorce
> 'Twixt natural son and sire ! thou bright defiler

Of Hymen's purest bed ! thou valiant Mars !
Thou ever young, fresh, lov'd, and delicate wooer,
Whose blush doth thaw the consecrated snow
That lies on Dian's lap ! thou visible god,
That solder'st close impossibilities,
And mak'st them kiss ! that speak'st with every tongue,
To every purpose ! O thou touch of hearts !
Think, thy slave man rebels, and by thy virtue
Set them into confounding odds, that beasts
May have the world in empire.

(IV. iii. 384.)

' Beasts '. All Shakespeare's work aims variously at controlling, fighting, or, at the best, using, the ' beast ' in man. His Saint George takes different forms, but the conflict of man's high spiritual aristocracy and the various degrading shapes that so easily usurp power is recurrent. Greed is here the ' beast '. Disgusted, Timon imprecates all possible disorders on a civilisation that has severed contact with the foundations of all true order : emotional sincerity, generosity, nobility. A certain sovereign essence has been wronged. *Measure for Measure* questions all temporal justice and authority; and *Troilus and Cressida* asserts the absolute necessity of degree and order. But Timon personifies that indefinable essence of generosity and grace on which all such arguments pivot. The gold he gives to all who visit him may be allowed to symbolise the golden wisdom that burns alike in his early love and later hate. Here Shakespeare attacks a society, and that means, to him, England, for insincerity, for not being true to itself, for selling its own nobility and generosity, its own best human and therefore royal excellence, its highest purpose on earth. If Shakespeare finally takes his stand, as he does, by England's destiny, he has certainly shirked nothing of such criticisms as those levelled in our own day by pacifist and communist. Timon is, indeed, even more than a critic of society. He is the soul of great poetry voyaging on a lonely quest, most truly at home with sun and moon and earth and all elements of nature, and listening from time to time to the sob and surge of the great seas into which his story fades. From the depths of eternity he pronounces judgment on the pettiness of man.

It may seem strange, even rash, to search for any national

message in such tragedies as *King Lear* and *Macbeth*. I make no attempt here to characterise the racked universe of the one or the demonic energies of the other. The two plays dig at the roots of evil, seeing political disruption as closely related respectively to (i) family disunion, and (ii) psychic disease and dark forces of the immaterial world. There is therefore a continuity, of a general kind, with our other political studies concentrating on order and disorder, and any explicit references to England fall accordingly into place.

Remember how important to Shakespeare is the unity, which is, also, the sincerity, of England; and how his history cycle shows the turmoils of civil war leading towards Tudor supremacy. Now Lear is king of Britain; and he is old. In old age he gives up his sovereignty in all but name, sentimentally wishing for ease, with his three daughters dividing the realm; just as Great Britain, in our time, has appeared old, has tried to relinquish that power that is yet her pressing destiny, thinking to preserve her royalty on easy terms. Of his three children, two are wicked and deceitful, one sincere and good; and Lear foolishly banishes the youngest, Cordelia, together with the loyal Kent, for an outspoken sincerity, the virtue to Shakespeare of all the most important, only to learn, at terrible cost, his mistake. I shall of course make no attempt to equate Goneril, Regan, and Cordelia with any specific tendencies of the modern world; but would merely point to Great Britain's too-ready relaxation of responsibility within and without her own national limits, her contentment with a rash disunity, and her denying, to-day and often in the past, that dearest, and deepest, soul-possession my essay labours to define. There is nothing strange in all this. Reference to Britain becomes explicit in an unfortunately obscure piece of doggerel spoken by the Fool, purporting half-mockingly to describe the conditions of the country's future disintegration, and ending:

> Then shall the realm of Albion
> Come to great confusion.

(III. ii. 91.)

It is called a 'prophecy', and quite possibly the lines we have represent a comic actor's distortion of an original that appeared, in Shakespeare's day, meaningless. Or maybe Shakespeare's instinct enjoys using the Fool's inconsequence to push the play's dim national feeling into the twilight of a semi-conscious, semi-purposeful, prophetic commentary. Anyone who has read Sack-ville's *Gorboduc*, an earlier play on the theme of *Lear* with its precise reference, through dumb-show, of the plot to a nation, and in particular Britain, in disunity, or realises the fear of political disorder in the Elizabethan mind to which Dr. G. B. Harrison, on more strictly historical grounds, has called attention, will recog-nise how much more nationally important to Shakespeare than to the modern reader, unless duly warned, was a story about a king of Britain who relinquishes authority and paves the way for chaos.

The play is written, broadly, from a sense of oncoming disaster in Renaissance civilisation related to lack of family piety:

> These late eclipses in the sun and moon portend no good to us : though the wisdom of nature can reason it thus and thus, yet nature finds itself scourged by the sequent effects. Love cools, friendship falls off, brothers divide : in cities, mutinies; in countries, discord; in palaces, treason; and the bond cracked between son and father. This villain of mine comes under the prediction; there's son against father : the king falls from bias of nature; there's father against child. We have seen the best of our time : machinations, hollowness, treachery, and all ruinous disorders, follow us disquietly to our graves.
>
> (I. ii. 115.)

Like *Timon*, though less obviously, the play is a warning; and Lear's madness contains satire savage as Timon's, with a closely similar denunciation of civil justice. Another passage rouses an easy response today:

> If that the heavens do not their visible spirits
> Send quickly down to tame these vile offences,
> It will come,
> Humanity must perforce prey on itself,
> Like monsters of the deep.
>
> (IV. ii. 46.)

As in *Timon*, man's dangerous, lusting, brutality is compared, over and over again, to beasts; and in our last quotation they are water-beasts, like Tennyson's

> . . . dragons of the prime
> Which tear each other in their slime,

and the more apt, as in the Saint George legend, as symbols of unreclaimed instinct. These ugly forces Lear's original foolishness has unloosed, and Goneril and Regan and Edmund have their way, for a time. They regard the good people as weaklings, just as Germany regards England's respect for law and convention as a febrile symptom. So Goneril scorns her gentle husband Albany, while Edmund, the conscienceless, panther-like, villain, carries all before him. The evil people degenerate swiftly, growing worse and worse. They become sadistically brutal. But saving powers return with the love of Lear's youngest daughter Cordelia, as in *Macbeth* through child-innocence and a holy king. Shakespeare sets against Machiavellian intrigue (as with Edmund—a true descendant of Richard III), crude force, and all lustful evils, such simple champions of grace.

The power-quest and tyrannic ambitions explored in *Richard III* are in *Macbeth* presented at once more philosophically and more imaginatively, and both may contribute to our understanding of Hitler's Germany. According to Hermann Rauschning, Hitler must, like Lady Macbeth, have light by him continually. His unrestful dreams recall the nightmare and sleepless horrors so emphatic here. Macbeth's overriding will to self-realisation knows no limits:

> I conjure you, by that which you profess—
> Howe'er you come to know it—answer me :
> Though you untie the winds and let them fight
> Against the churches ; though the yesty waves
> Confound and swallow navigation up ;
> Though bladed corn be lodg'd and trees blown down ;
> Though castles topple on their warders' heads ;
> Though palaces and pyramids do slope
> Their heads to their foundations ; though the treasure
> Of Nature's germens tumble all together,
> Even till destruction sicken ; answer me
> To what I ask you.

> (IV. i. 50.)

This is spoken to the Weird Women whom Macbeth visits to learn his future : Hitler has, too, his astrologers and crystal-gazers. In the depths of the human soul superstition and tyranny are one. Ross tells of the havoc ravaging Scotland under this nightmare rule :

.'. . . Alas ! poor country ;
Almost afraid to know itself.   It cannot
Be call'd our mother, but our grave ; where nothing,
But who knows nothing, is once seen to smile ;
Where sighs and groans and shrieks that rent the air
Are made, not mark'd ; where violent sorrow seems
A modern ecstasy ; the dead man's knell
Is there scarce ask'd for who ; and good men's lives
Expire before the flowers in their caps,
Dying or ere they sicken.

                                        (IV. iii. 164.)

Macbeth's mad and useless murders make Scotland a shambles.
Like Hitler's Germany, he has spies everywhere: ' There's not
a one of them but in his house I keep a servant fee'd ' (III. iv. 131).
This is no twisting of great poetry to serve contemporary propaganda.   Shakespeare's *Richard III*, *Lear* and *Macbeth* isolate and
intensify certain negative essences of the will to power, accompanied freely by deception and slaughter, which Hitler would himself admit to exist within his own drama.   Indeed, he claims them
as part of his genius, deliberately putting into practice, according
to Rauschning, what would be ' crime ' within a civil order,
urging, with some justice, that great changes are always so con-
ditioned.   Therefore to equate, provisionally, Macbeth with Hitler
is perfectly legitimate, and wrongs neither.

However that may be, and however irresistible the evil forces
may seem, Shakespeare clearly defines the opposing powers of
good.   We have, first, the good King Duncan, whose murder is
Macbeth's original crime:

                        Besides, this Duncan
Hath borne his faculties so meek, hath been
So clear in his great office, that his virtues
Will plead like angels trumpet-tongu'd against
The deep damnation of his taking-off ;
And pity, like a naked new-born babe,
Striding the blast, or heaven's cherubin, hors'd
Upon the sightless couriers of the air,
Shall blow the horrid deed in every eye,
That tears shall drown the wind.   I have no spur
To prick the sides of my intent, but only
Vaulting ambition.

                                        (I. vii. 16.)

Compare with this the vision shown Macbeth by the Weird Sisters of a power combining child-purity (as in our ' naked new-born babe '), nature and sovereignty, a combination which, at long last, must win.   The apparition is ' a child crowned, with a tree in his hand ', and Macbeth addresses it:

> What is this
> That rises like the issue of a king,
> And wears upon his baby-brow the round
> And top of sovereignty ?
>
> (IV. i. 86.)

In strong contrast is the other apparition, the ' armed head ', iron force severed from its body, the destructive and self-destructive essence.

Now the witches have prophesied that the descendants of Banquo shall rule after him.   His own kingship is lustful and possessive, Banquo's un-selfseeking and creative;   his doomed to wither, Banquo's destined to immortality.   The thought of this torments Macbeth, who expresses his fears in a soliloquy condensing vividly the essential insecurity and uneasiness of a tyrannous rule:

> To be thus is nothing ;
> But to be safely thus.   Our fears in Banquo
> Stick deep, and in his royalty of nature
> Reigns that which would be fear'd : 'tis much he dares,
> And, to that dauntless temper of his mind,
> He hath a wisdom that doth guide his valour
> To act in safety.   There is none but he
> Whose being I do fear ; and under him
> My genius is rebuk'd, as it is said
> Mark Antony's was by Caesar.   He chid the sisters
> When first they put the name of king upon me,
> And bade them speak to him ; then, prophet-like,
> They hail'd him father to a line of kings.
> Upon my head they plac'd a fruitless crown,
> And put a barren sceptre in my gripe,
> Thence to be wrench'd with an unlineal hand,
> No son of mine succeeding.   If't be so,
> For Banquo's issue have I fil'd my mind ;
> For them the gracious Duncan have I murder'd ;
> Put rancours in the vessel of my peace
> Only for them ; and mine eternal jewel
> Given to the common enemy of man,

> To make them kings, the seed of Banquo kings !
> Rather than so, come fate into the list,
> And champion me to the utterance !
>
> (III. i. 48.)

He is further tormented by a vision of future Scottish kings blend-ing, after the union of realms under James I (during whose reign this play was written), into a line of English kings too; and the inevitable and expanding, organically growing, power suggested, together with those deep burnishings of a royal splendour so weighty throughout the poetry here, blend naturally into Shakespeare's general feeling elsewhere for England's, which is now also Scot-land's, undying sovereignty:

> Thou art too like the spirit of Banquo; down !
> Thy crown does sear mine eyeballs; and thy hair,
> Thou other gold-bound brow, is like the first :
> A third is like the former.   Filthy hags !
> Why do you show me this ?   A fourth !   Start, eyes !
> What ! will the line stretch out to the crack of doom ?
> Another yet ?   A seventh !   I'll see no more :
> And yet the eighth appears, who bears a glass
> Which shows me many more; and some I see
> That two-fold balls and treble sceptres carry.
> Horrible sight !   Now, I see 'tis true;
> For the blood-bolter'd Banquo smiles upon me,
> And points at them for his.
>
> (IV. i. 112.)

This line of kings is descended from Banquo, secure in an integrity that, in the midst of rampaging evil, can yet say:

> In the great hand of God I stand, and thence
> Against the undivulg'd pretence I fight
> Of treasonous malice.
>
> (II. iii. 137.)

In murdering Banquo, Macbeth tries to cut off Britain's future history at its root.   But Fleance escapes.

In Macbeth and Banquo two ways of serving both time and eternity are contrasted, and they cannot readily mix.   But notice that in this, Shakespeare's most profound dramatisation of evil, Great Britain's destiny is at stake.   This it is which wrestles with the power-lust and is shown, finally, as triumphant.   *Macbeth* points directly to *Henry VIII*.

E

The good powers are, moreover, definitely aligned with England. Thither the brave Macduff flies to join Malcolm, Scotland's true heir, and gather military assistance. A Scottish lord prays for angelic aid in his mission:

> Some holy angel
> Fly to the court of England and unfold
> His message ere he come, that a swift blessing
> May soon return to this our suffering country
> Under a hand accus'd !

(III. vi. 45.)

And what of that English court ? Here we have a scene of quiet, of peace, a backwater in the torrential action or a place where saving strength may be regarnered. Here too we have description of the holy English king, Edward the Confessor, and his miraculous powers against—how apt the name—a disease called ' the evil ':

Macduff : What's the disease he means ?
Malcolm :   'Tis call'd the evil :
> A most miraculous work in this good king,
> Which often, since my here-remain in England,
> I have seen him do. How he solicits heaven,
> Himself best knows ; but strangely-visited people,
> All swoln and ulcerous, pitiful to the eye,
> The mere despair of surgery, he cures ;
> Hanging a golden stamp about their necks,
> Put on with holy prayers ; and 'tis spoken
> To the succeeding royalty he leaves
> The healing benediction. With this strange virtue,
> He hath a heavenly gift of prophecy,
> And sundry blessings hang about his throne
> That speak him full of grace.

(IV. iii. 146.)

In a yet wider sense something of that heritage may yet remain. So Macduff and Malcolm with an English army led by old Siward— ' an older and a better soldier none that Christendom gives out ' (IV. iii. 191)—set forth to conquer tyranny, with the aid of Birnam wood, all nature joining in the cause. Pushing through this play's structure rise, from the murk and nightmare, solid shapes of a blessed power, with baby innocence and gentle nature as invincible allies, crowned by an English king as defender of righteousness and mediator of grace.

There are, of course, many more implications in such plays as *King Lear* and *Macbeth* than I can here discuss. Notice how in all these greater plays the more spiritual conflict objectifies itself into armed opposition, with a final re-establishment of order, as in *Hamlet* and *Timon* with Fortinbras and Alcibiades as arbiters. We can, however, notice also that in all some obvious outward shape of nobility, kingly rank or fine soldiership—the tragic hero, even Hamlet, is always a soldierly figure—is overthrown by an emotional force partly at least touching some family, and especially feminine, relationship; for we must not forget the part played by Lady Macbeth. This pattern is very clear in such a play as *Othello*, wherein a great soldier is brought to ruin by the Machiavellian intrigues of the villainous Iago, who raises in him a violent and agonised distrust of his lately married, and deeply faithful, wife, Desdemona. In the middle-action, as despair overwhelms him, Othello recalls his soldierly glory:

> I had been happy, if the general camp,
> Pioners and all, had tasted her sweet body,
> So I had nothing known. O! now, for ever
> Farewell the tranquil mind; farewell content!
> Farewell the plumed troop and the big wars
> That make ambition virtue! O, farewell!
> Farewell the neighing steed, and the shrill trump,
> The spirit-stirring drum, the ear-piercing fife,
> The royal banner, and all quality,
> Pride, pomp, and circumstance of glorious war!
> And, O you mortal engines, whose rude throats
> The immortal Jove's dread clamours counterfeit,
> Farewell! Othello's occupation's gone!

(III. iii. 346.)

This overthrowing of what might be termed a masculine value by a more feminine force may be referred to those numerous women throughout the Histories standing in the background of martial action and political rivalry, variously watching, often suffering for and sometimes condemning, as from a deeper wisdom, man's turbulent and ambitious drama. The process is one aspect of Shakespeare's spiritualised and tragic understanding of all temporal power; and it is precisely this that, in the long run, renders whatever military fervours or national gospel he may offer so peculiarly invulnerable. There are always cosmic powers waiting to shatter the brittle outside of over-confident and insubstantial appearance, and the rights Shakespeare ultimately believes in are only those which themselves derive sanction from this cosmic source, which becomes, at the limit, as with the English king in *Macbeth*, divine grace. With this tendency in mind let us glance shortly at *Antony and Cleopatra* and *Coriolanus*, in both of which soldierly pride is contrasted with a feminine allegiance.

As in *Julius Caesar*, we must be prepared to see in all Shakespeare's Roman studies a full flood of contemporary feeling. Rome was to the Elizabethan a prototype and an exemplar. The issues raised in *Julius Caesar* of monarchy and freedom, of personal and symbolic sovereignty, Caesar the man and Caesar the spirit of imperial guidance, all have close, Tudor, implications. And so, when in *Antony and Cleopatra* one of Rome's joint imperial rulers throws away all soldierly honour and imperial sway for a woman's love, we have Shakespeare at work on a vital conflict. Without shirking the tragedy of Antony's fall, he expends his art lavishly on the cosmic powers of a great love; while his Cleopatra, into whom all his feminine understanding is condensed, is so amazing a creation that one is scarcely surprised at her victory. No Shakespearian hero, not even Othello, is so idealised in point of soldierly valour as Antony. He incorporates at its pagan best the primitive energies, and is therefore compared naturally to that golden and kingly beast, the lion, in contradistinction to the tyrant Macbeth, who is, at a somewhat similar moment, imaged as a 'bear'. Antony is a mighty oak of a man, a vast strength uprooted, and crashes in magnificent and rebounding echoes of poetry. The disrupting force is Cleopatra. He is masculinity personified, she expressly and universally feminine, with all peculiarly feminine wiles of grace, merriment, fascination, courage, weakness and, above and justifying, lending meaning to, all, love. She is, too, queen of Egypt: the play scintillates with splendours and, while an empire is split by civil war, love's presence itself assumes imperial stature. Beside Romeo's dream of re-union beyond death with its ' I revived and was an emperor ' (V. i. 9) we may place Cleopatra's dream: ' I dream'd there was an Emperor Antony . . .' (V. ii. 76). We all but reach an equation of love and empire,

just as Shakespeare's royalism holds always something of an erotic
potency.   In this golden play both soldierly honour and love
blaze with noonday strength; and, though love wins, and seems
to lift the lovers beyond death to realms of eternal fruition, the
two values are once, for a superb moment, as once also in *Othello*,
felt as identical, and both are contrasted with the cool and cal-
culating policy of Caesar.   The general reference to Shakespeare's
refusal of all simple solutions is obvious.

We should notice, too, the play's amazing stress on loyalty,
even though unwise.   Enobarbus deserts his master at a crucial
moment, and with sound reasons for doing so.   Nevertheless swift
retribution overtakes him, not from without, but, in typical
Shakespearian fashion, from within:

> I am alone the villain of the earth,
> And feel I am so most.   O Antony !
> Thou mine of bounty, how wouldst thou have paid
> My better service, when my turpitude
> Thou dost so crown with gold !   This blows my heart :
> If swift thought break it not, a swifter mean
> Shall outstrike thought; but thought will do't, I feel.
> I fight against thee !   No : I will go seek
> Some ditch, wherein to die ; the foul'st best fits
> My latter part of life.
>
>   (IV. vi. 29.)

And again, at point of death:

>   O Antony !
> Nobler than my revolt is infamous,
> Forgive me in thine own particular ;
> But let the world rank me in register
> A master-leaver and a fugitive.
> O Antony !   O Antony !
>
>   (IV. ix. 18.)

Think back to Henry V's words to those treacherous lords, Cam-
bridge, Scroop, and Grey; to the deep respect always accorded
loyalty in Shakespeare, as with Kent in *King Lear*; and then
consider the many recent examples of a wider, more national,
treachery, in various European countries, and, indeed, in our own
thinking during the last two decades.   There are, surely, certain
unreasoned loyalties—and a reasoned loyalty is scarcely such at

all—to a master not faultless, any more than Antony was fault-less, yet which we must, at peril not only of swift disaster but also of self-condemnation, acknowledge.

Coriolanus strikes home, as does no other play, to our most pressing contemporary horror: the horror of stark, unadulterated, militarism. Coriolanus is brought up by that stern Roman matron, Volumnia, his devoted mother, to honour, not Rome, but ' honour ' itself, to be a veritable superman of a soldier. Both Coriolanus and Volumnia sin through pride and excessive concen-tration on an ambition which, if allowed to become an end in itself, proves suicidal. Warfare is shown as harsh, brutal, thun-derous in impact, and Coriolanus stands as the honoured expert in its grim technique. All that Germany most admires is in the man; and, pathetically, his mother welcomes him home, for-getting, as we are reminded, the women of Corioli whom his success has left widowed or sonless.

But Volumnia has created something she cannot control, and Coriolanus' pride becomes intolerable. We see now that he warred only for ' honour '; for himself, not for Rome. Whoever puts an abstraction, a word, an ideology, before his God, his country, or his family, vital allegiances that may indeed themselves conflict but are all alike hostile to those insidious abstract virtues, whether they call themselves ' honour ' or ' reason ', and to what-ever particular ' -isms ' they may lead, may be, at the limit, found guilty of an ego-centric idolatry. But against that little ego stands a greater self in us all; and that greater self, as with Enobarbus, awaits its time. Coriolanus' pride refuses compromise; Rome finds him intolerable, his mother pathetically attempts to retrieve the error of his upbringing; he is banished.

Now the inherent paradox of the elevation of warrior-honour to a supreme value is driven home. Nursing his wounded pride, Coriolanus leads his one-time enemies against his own city. En-camped outside its walls, he has Rome at his mercy, and expects soon to taste the sweets of revenge. As a last hope, Rome sends his own mother, wife, and child to soften, if they may, his im-placable will. It seems a forlorn hope. Here he is in his iron, dictatorial, dignity as described by the witty old aristocrat, Mene-nius:

Sicinius : Is't possible that so short a time can alter the condition of a man?

Menenius : There is differency between a grub and a butterfly; yet your butterfly was a grub. This Marcius is grown from man to dragon : he has wings; he's more than a creeping thing.

Sicinius : He loved his mother dearly.

Menenius : So did he me; and he no more remembers his mother now than an eight-year-old horse. The tartness of his face sours ripe grapes : when he walks, he moves like an engine, and the ground shrinks before his treading; he is able to pierce a corslet with his eye; talks like a knell, and his hum is a battery. He sits in his state, as a thing made for Alexander. What he bids be done is finished with his bidding. He wants nothing of a god but eternity and a heaven to throne in.

Sicinius : Yes, mercy, if you report him truly.

Menenius : I paint him in the character. Mark what mercy his mother shall bring from him : there is no more mercy in him than there is milk in a male tiger; that shall our poor city find.

(V. iv. 10.)

This is Shakespeare's mature commentary on all heartless devotees of military honour, men like Hotspur and Tybalt, a type of which Homer's Achilles is an ancient literary example, and Hitler and Mussolini contemporary grand-scale exponents. See how Coriolanus has become inhuman; he is a 'dragon', or 'tiger'; or rather worse, a machine, a robot, almost un-alive. There is an implied criticism of pride and force corresponding to that in the 'armed head' apparition in *Macbeth*, wherein violent destructiveness is shown as both threatening and severed from its organic body, and therefore rootless as well as sapless. In the same way, Coriolanus' pride is now shown as self-contradictory and suicidal.

His mother, wife, and son approach him. He stands firm and will not obey 'instinct' (V. iii. 35), already half-confessing that his deepest self rejects his self-nursed ideal. When his own mother kneels to him, it seems like a 'pebble' on the beach insulting the stars, a 'cedar' striking the sun (V. iii. 56–62): for his pride is a little, earthly thing, and his love for his mother a great cosmic power. Yet he will not give way. Volumnia speaks scathingly, scornfully, of his treacherous intention, and, since his long story of pride derived first from an inborn desire to deserve his mother's praise, her scorn now, a voice drawing power from his deepest childhood, disarms him.   He ' holds her hand in silence ', and then:

> O, mother, mother !
> What have you done ?   Behold ! the heavens do ope,
> The gods look down, and this unnatural scene
> They laugh at.   O my mother ! mother ! O !
> You have won a happy victory to Rome ;
> But, for your son, believe it, O ! believe it,
> Most dangerously you have with him prevail'd,
> If not most mortal to him.

(V. iii. 182.)

She wins, unconditionally.   At once this hard, stony, play brightens, and after four acts of city imagery and warlike sickening thuds and clamours and pride of unbending iron, suddenly the sun blazes and music sounds.   Coriolanus cannot live out to the end this inhuman thing he has worshipped, his own self, as with Achilles before Priam, rejecting his lonely, barren, quest of honour.   So, too, in the wider issues of our day, Fascism and Nazism distort human nature itself, which will rise and reject those infertile values unsanctioned by the deeper powers.   The softer, more feminine, more filial and parental, virtues may be, for a while, dormant, but await their turn; and ' mercy ', as Sicinius suggests, remains basic to divine ordinance.

Towards the end of his life Shakespeare composed a series of plays deeply tinged with religious mysticism, as though the profundities of spiritual experience reached in the great tragedies had forced his genius on to a realisation of mystic wisdom and mysterious resurrection beyond death.   Such plays are *Pericles* and *The Winter's Tale*.   All along Shakespeare's historic and temporal analysis has been closely aware of life's tragedy, though at the same time recognising the necessity, compulsion, of noble effort in terms of this human world.   But in *Antony and Cleopatra* the tragic defeat itself becomes a sublime victory; and at the end of Shakespeare's writing career this spiritual insight grows positive and assured, as in the bringing back to life of Thaisa, Pericles' queen, by the saintly Cerimon, and the miraculous resurrection of Hermione, supposed dead, at the close of *The Winter's Tale*. There is, too, a strangely sweet concentration on youth, with the recovery of long-lost, royal, children, as in the wondrous return of

Marina to her careworn father King Pericles, and the equally amazing restoration of Perdita. Now how does this last mode react on Shakespeare's more directly political and national message ?

The best known of these plays is *The Tempest*. It is obviously a symbolic work, whose fantasy-structure is used to sum up the inward meanings of the long spiritual pilgrimage of the great plays. Prospero, formerly Duke of Milan, and somewhat too studious, like the Duke in *Measure for Measure*, for that office, has been supplanted by a wicked brother and cast adrift on the ocean to live as best he may a marooned existence, with his daughter Miranda, on an island. Here he pursues his studies, grows powerful in natural magic, and gets two semi-human creatures, Caliban and Ariel, representative figures of animal and spiritual energy, to serve his purposes. At last he charms his enemies to the island, overpowers and forgives them, renounces his magic and returns to re-engage his ducal responsibilities at Milan. What are we to make of this queer story ?

First, we can see an obvious re-working of *Measure for Measure*, with mystic wisdom replacing psychological insight. The two dukes are, however, really the same man, and both plays are working over that age-old problem of the philosopher king. Surely, one feels, the wisest type of man should govern, and yet that type inevitably finds government and temporal magnificence repellent, as does Cerimon, the saintly recluse of *Pericles*:

> I hold it ever,
> Virtue and cunning were endowments greater
> Than nobleness and riches ; careless heirs
> May the two latter darken and expend ;
> But immortality attends the former
> Making a man a god.
>
> (III. ii. 26.)

Our minds are thrown back on Shakespeare's religious Henry VI and impractical but, as his story grows tragic, deeply mystical, Richard II. Prospero is, too, together with Ariel and Caliban, an obvious repetition of much in Timon. Timon splits now into three persons. Both Timon and Prospero are driven by human ingratitude to a cave by the wild sea; Timon's spiritual aspiration and prophetic denunciations are in Ariel; while his return to naked savagery has its parallel in Caliban. Here is Ariel's accusation of Prospero's enemies, now helpless on the island, which may be read as an accusation of all societies who have wronged their truest good, their highest national possession, as Athens wrongs Timon and Milan Prospero:

> You are three men of sin, whom Destiny—
> That hath to instrument this lower world
> And what is in't—the never-surfeited sea
> Hath caused to belch up you; and on this island
> Where man doth not inhabit; you 'mongst men
> Being most unfit to live. I have made you mad;
> And even with such-like valour men hang and drown
> Their proper selves. You fools! I and my fellows
> Are ministers of fate: the elements
> Of whom your swords are temper'd, may as well
> Wound the loud winds, or with bemock'd-at stabs
> Kill the still-closing waters, as diminish
> One dowle that's in my plume; my fellow-ministers
> Are like invulnerable. If you could hurt,
> Your swords are now too massy for your strengths,
> And will not be uplifted. But, remember—
> For that's my business to you—that you three
> From Milan did supplant good Prospero;
> Expos'd unto the sea, which hath requit it,
> Him and his innocent child: for which foul deed
> The powers, delaying, not forgetting, have
> Incens'd the seas and shores, yea, all the creatures,
> Against your peace. Thee of thy son, Alonso,
> They have bereft; and do pronounce, by me,
> Lingering perdition—worse than any death
> Can be at once—shall step by step attend
> You and your ways; whose wraths to guard you from—
> Which here in this most desolate isle, else falls
> Upon your heads—is nothing but heart-sorrow
> And a clear life ensuing.
>
> (III. iii. 53.)

Earlier tragic discords are, very clearly, constituent to that inclusive harmony which *The Tempest* aims to define: the suffering Alonso searching for his child repeats the purgatory of Lear, while Sebastian and Antonio together act a miniature *Macbeth*. Prospero, like Lear, Pericles and Leontes (in *The Winter's Tale*), has a treasured daughter saved from the storms of chance. Miranda is threatened, but kept intact, and never lost, Prospero's wise guardianship differentiating him from the follies of former monarchs. Ariel's speech is spoken for all states at all times. Remember the poetic condemnation Shakespeare accorded those who too lightly thought to desecrate a Richard's kingly person. Something there is which we too, in our time, have scorned and cast out of our city, some Timon who might save us in the hour of peril, some Prospero of magical insight, some ruling power of wisdom and goodness; and a mighty sovereignty remains dethroned.

That sovereignty is not purely secular and rational, but rather mystic and poetic. It is both stern and loving. Prospero controls his Ariel and Caliban as man's judgment must control both ethereal fancy and physical instinct. Caliban is a half-fish, a monster both watery and earthy, a semi-devil, and must be referred to those numerous beasts throughout Shakespeare denoting an energy which, if allowed to distort human graciousness, gives us the 'cacodemon' Richard III, the 'dragon' Coriolanus, and the 'monsters of the deep' in *Lear*: while a close relationship, through his mother Sycorax, to black magic points also to *Macbeth*. Bur Prospero is the wise governor, the philosopher king; and his stern, almost brutal, repression of Caliban, to whom the poet has nevertheless devoted a most exquisite creative sympathy, is in tone with Shakespeare's ethical self-control throughout his excursions among demonic, and often imaginatively attractive, energies; a control which distinguishes Shakespeare from the more Germanic artist or philosopher, to whom energy, as such, tends to claim highest honours. And what of Miranda, Prospero's daughter? I think she suggests a human purity to be saved, guarded, and when the time is ripe restored, to redeem with her natural and unspoilt grace a sin-struck society.

Prospero lives half in eternity, and from that eminence sees beyond all temporal glories whatsoever, as, indeed, did Richard II and Henry V, but presses yet further, beyond Macbeth (in his 'Tomorrow' speech) and Timon, into the transience of the created universe itself:

> These our actors,
> As I foretold you, were all spirits and
> Are melted into air, into thin air :

And, like the baseless fabric of this vision,
The cloud-capp'd towers, the gorgeous palaces,
The solemn temples, the great globe itself,
Yea, all which it inherit, shall dissolve
And, like this insubstantial pageant faded,
Leave not a rack behind.   We are such stuff
As dreams are made on, and our little life
Is rounded with a sleep.

(IV. i. 148.)

Yet, though living within the consciousness of such deep, though not bitter, wisdom, Prospero finally *returns to Milan*, and takes up again his practical duties.

Prospero's renunciation of magic powers has often enough been considered the poet's autobiographical farewell to his literary career.   It is that.   But *The Tempest* is not, as is popularly supposed, Shakespeare's last play; and, just as Prospero, the poet-seer, returns to his ducal office, so Shakespeare, after a long line of outwardly non-historical plays, plays not obviously concerned with England's destiny at all, yet each, as I have shown, closely concerned with the deepest and darkest issues raised by consideration of that destiny in his earlier work, after all this, Shakespeare writes, as his last play, *Henry VIII*.   His bark has come to harbour.   He returns to a national theme, set nearer his own day than any previous attempt, and deeply loads it with orthodox Christian feeling.   Here the extravagances and profundities of the great sequence come, at the last, to rest.

V

MAIDEN PHOENIX

Before, however, approaching *Henry VIII*, we must consider *Cymbeline*, written probably just before *The Tempest*. Here we find the not-too-obvious national interest of such works as *King Lear* and *Macbeth* maturing into a more explicit message, though the historic setting is, like theirs, ancient. Study of it should certainly make my remarks on those other plays appear less bold. Now, since a major purpose of *Cymbeline* is to celebrate the union of Rome and Britain, we must, for a moment, return our thoughts to Rome and all that it signified to Shakespeare.

Ancient Rome loomed vaster in Shakespeare's national imagination than it does in ours. If we turn to any Elizabethan writer—say, for example, the essays of Lord Bacon—we find him referring continually to incidents from Roman, or Greek, history, as well as quoting from classic authors. Alexander and Julius Caesar are recognised giants, prototypes of military conquest and imperial greatness: see how Hamlet introduces them into his graveyard meditations. In *Julius Caesar*, written probably about the time of *Hamlet*, Shakespeare feels into what is, to him, a key-moment in man's existence. Roman history, with its early liberation from tyranny and subsequent commonwealth, the dictatorial powers of Caesar, and the imperial Rome that followed, raises all possible questions of government. Most of the political complexities, involving both republican and monarchical conceptions, of modern Europe are embryonic in Shakespeare's play. The cause of liberty solicits, through Brutus, who looks back to his ancestor, the liberator of Rome from its early tyranny, our approval; but revolution, as such, is felt as only provisionally successful, the 'spirit' of Caesar winning after his death. The old conflict of *Richard II* is here given a far subtler presentation. Caesar is not yet king and cannot claim divine office. Shall he be assassinated to prevent tyranny? Is kingship, as such, good or bad? Caesar is, as it were, the essence of kingship, though not yet king; and yet again, weak, puny, as a man. As the plunging of Brutus' dagger into his body approaches, it is as though history itself quivers, totters, is itself gashed open, exposing ruinous self-conflict above the streets of Rome :

> Fierce fiery warriors fought upon the clouds,
> In ranks and squadrons and right form of war,
> Which drizzled blood upon the Capitol ;
> The noise of battle hurtled in the air . . .
>
> (II. ii. 19.)

One almost feels the shadow of modern aerial combat across the Shakespearian page.   After the murder Antony prophecies war·

> Woe to the hand that shed this costly blood !
> Over thy wounds now do I prophesy,
> Which like dumb mouths do ope their ruby lips,
> To beg the voice and utterance of my tongue,
> A curse shall light upon the limbs of men ;
> Domestic fury and fierce civil strife
> Shall cumber all the parts of Italy ;
> Blood and destruction shall be so in use,
> And dreadful objects so familiar,
> That mothers shall but smile when they behold
> Their infants quarter'd with the hands of war ;
> All pity chok'd with custom of fell deeds :
> And Caesar's spirit, ranging for revenge,
> With Ate by his side come hot from hell,
> Shall in these confines with a monarch's voice
> Cry ' Havoc ! ' and let slip the dogs of war ;
> That this foul deed shall smell above the earth
> With carrion men, groaning for burial.
>
> (III. i. 258.)

Nowhere is Shakespeare's trust in essential sovereignty more vivid. In spite of nerve-racking cataclysm and murder, in spite of his own triviality as a man, in spite of Brutus' noble republicanism, the spirit of Caesar is yet all-potent:

> O Julius Caesar ! thou art mighty yet !
> Thy spirit walks abroad, and turns our swords
> In our own proper entrails.
>
> (V. iii. 94.)

In opposing the Caesarean essence—and it is that, the ' spirit ', not merely the body, of Caesar they aim at, as a speech of Brutus asserts—the conspirators merely slay themselves, while that spirit moves on, indestructible. They aim, and it is the root-error of many a revolutionary, to slay not a man only but royalty itself; which must not, and indeed cannot, be done. Here all Shakespeare's thought and feeling on political discord, government, human history itself, is compacted, distilled, and rendered in a dynamic tension of opposites, above which some vague, undefined, imperial splendour stands like a Colossus.

We have already seen how both *Antony and Cleopatra* and *Coriolanus* are relevant to our discussion, with a relevance not to be distinguished with any finality from their Roman settings. It is the Roman Empire, with all that that means, which Antony barters for a supreme love, while Coriolanus' mother is a stern Roman matron who drives the Spartan pride of her kind beyond the limits of nobility. And this is my present, and all-important, point, without a clear understanding of which *Cymbeline* is a nearly meaningless play: Shakespeare, at the youth of Great Britain's imperial history, is necessarily fascinated by the accomplished imperialism of ancient Rome. He feels England now as inheriting the great destiny of Rome, with new strength incorporated from the centuries of Christendom. If any doubts about this remain, let us turn to his early play, *Titus Andronicus*. The story is set late in Rome's imperial history—and how neatly Shakespeare's four Roman plays cover the main periods of that history—and starts with noble phrases:

> I am his first-born son that was the last
> That wore the imperial diadem of Rome . . .
>
> (I. i. 5.)

The political purity of ' royal Rome ' must be maintained:

> And suffer not dishonour to approach
> The imperial seat, to virtue consecrate,
> To justice, continence, and nobility;
> But let desert in pure election shine,
> And, Romans, fight for freedom in your choice.
>
> (I. i. 13.)

That is, precisely, what Shakespeare feels about England also. The action shows intrigue, faction, and hideous wrongs hatched by Tamora, queen of the Goths, and Aaron, the Moor. As usual, the evil is felt as bestial, and of Tamora, in the final speech, it is said, ' Her life was beast-like and devoid of pity ' (V. iii. 199); for pity is constituent to Shakespeare's sense of greatness in man or nation. In fairness we must, however, observe that she originally suffers from the cruel slaughter of her own son, and herself implores mercy in true Shakespearian manner:

> But must my sons be slaughter'd in the streets
> For valiant doings in their country's cause?
> O! if to fight for king and commonweal
> Were piety in thine, it is in these.
> Andronicus, stain not thy tomb with blood:
> Wilt thou draw near the nature of the gods?
> Draw near them then in being merciful;
> Sweet mercy is nobility's true badge:
> Thrice-noble Titus, spare my first-born son.
>
> (I. i. 112.)

The action dramatises her revenge, leading to many horrors; but we return at the last to sanity, and a speech near the play's conclusion closely recalls both the final speech of *King John* and John of Gaunt's prophecy in *Richard II*:

> You sad-fac'd men, people and sons of Rome,
> By uproar sever'd, like a flight of fowl
> Scatter'd by winds and high tempestuous gusts,
> O! let me teach you how to knit again
> This scatter'd corn into one mutual sheaf,
> These broken limbs again into one body;
> Lest Rome herself be bane unto herself,
> And she whom mighty kingdoms curtsy to,
> Like a forlorn and desperate castaway,
> Do shameful execution on herself.
>
> (V. iii. 67.)

Here is the very accent of Shakespeare's words on England, for to him Rome and England are all but spiritually identical. Now *Cymbeline*, which, we must remember, is one of Shakespeare's latest plays, carefully dramatises a union of Rome and Britain.

It is a complicated work with many strands interweaving. My notice must be brief, and I shall select carefully for my purpose. The two sons of King Cymbeline have been absconded in childhood and brought up by a banished, but really faithful, lord, like

Kent in *King Lear*, among wild Welsh mountains. They live in a cave, ignorant, like Miranda, of their high birth, in close contact with nature, hunting and paying honour to the sun, adoring the heavens as 'a morning's holy office' (III. iii. 4). 'Hail, heaven!' they cry in turn (III. iii. 9). They have animal strength and pagan piety, but in them nature is itself half divine, and their deepest instincts are normally as gentle as that 'modest stillness and humility' King Henry counselled as most worthy in times of peace, though, on occasion, they can show the tiger strain he urged as best suited for war:

> O thou goddess!
> Thou divine Nature, how thyself thou blazon'st
> In these two princely boys. They are as gentle
> As zephyrs, blowing below the violet,
> Not wagging his sweet head; and yet as rough,
> Their royal blood enchaf'd, as the rud'st wind,
> That by the top doth take the mountain pine,
> And make him stoop to the vale. 'Tis wonder
> That an invisible instinct should frame them
> To royalty unlearn'd, honour untaught,
> Civility not seen from other, valour
> That wildly grows in them, but yields a crop
> As if it had been sow'd!
>
> (IV. ii. 169.)

At the last, they are restored to Cymbeline. What are they? What must they mean to us? They represent strength with gentleness, possessing what must, indeed, seem a semi-pagan virility with yet an innate sweetness. It is, I think, something we do not easily, to-day, understand; but it is something which England must, and perhaps England best can, create, or awake, or may be only recapture. They are 'princely' boys; and that word 'princely' alone saves the conception from any dangerous paganism, distinguishing them from all ruthless acts or brutal assertion. I think Germany to-day glimpses, and reaches after, their quality, but with one, all-important, blind spot in her understanding, from which the Shakespearian feeling for true, innate sovereignty alone can save us, or her. For such sovereignty is a deeply religious thing, with a grand humility and wide generosity. These are the long-lost boys who are given back to Cymbeline,

F

King of Britain, as the troubled action dissolves in national accord:
'Now these her princes are come home again . . .'

The fortunes of Posthumus Leonatus, the centre of dramatic
interest, involve his separation from Imogen, his newly-married
wife and daughter of the King; his deception by Iachimo, a close
cousin of Iago in *Othello*, who intrigues to make him distrust and
attempt to slay his wife; and, finally, his recognition of error and
re-enjoyment of love. This loss of faith in matters of love indeed
beats throughout Shakespeare: in *Troilus and Cressida*, *Othello*,
Timon, continually. Sometimes the distrust is justified, sometimes
erroneous, but, generally, we can say that Shakespeare is trying
to incorporate the full riches of the erotic instinct in a final inviol-
able integrity. Therefore, just as in *King Lear* lack of family
piety is related to national discord, so Posthumus' story blends
with the recovery of the two sons of Cymbeline, and all that that
suggests, into the play's more national structure. This is made
clear by the prophetic tablet left by Jupiter, king of the gods, after
visiting Posthumus in sleep:

> Whenas a lion's whelp shall, to himself unknown, without seeking
> find, and be embraced by a piece of tender air; and when from a
> stately cedar shall be lopped branches, which, being dead many
> years, shall after revive, be jointed to the old stock, and freshly
> grow: then shall Posthumus end his miseries, Britain be fortunate,
> and flourish in peace and plenty.
>
> (V. iv. 138.)

The 'lion's whelp' is, according to the Soothsayer, Posthumus
Leonatus, and Imogen the 'piece of tender air'; the union
suggested, as the Soothsayer's words help to emphasise, being
that of strength with spiritual sincerity, manliness with womanly
gentleness. The stately cedar, which is a favourite Shakespearian
symbol of steadfast power (as at *2 Henry VI*, V. i. 205; *3 Henry VI*,
V. ii. 11), and which we shall meet again in *Henry VIII*, is Cymbeline, and the branches his princely sons. See how Posthumus'
story, reflecting Shakespeare's long concern with man as an individual, dovetails with the wider national, and semi-allegorical,
prophecy, whose oracular manner recalls Lyly's *Endimion*.

The Romans are fighting the British for the tribute King
Cymbeline has neglected to pay. Though Iachimo, 'slight thing

of Italy ', is to be felt as a Renaissance creature of contemporary, Machiavellian, intrigue, the Roman army and ' imperial Caesar ' are of the ancient world. The use of anachronism appears deliberate, pointing an important contrast. Now the Soothsayer who interprets the tablet had a vision of his own concerning the fighting:

> Last night the very gods show'd me a vision—
> I fast and pray'd for their intelligence—thus :
> I saw Jove's bird, the Roman eagle, wing'd
> From the spongy south to this part of the west,
> There vanish'd in the sunbeams ; which portends,
> Unless my sins abuse my divination,
> Success to the Roman host.
>
> (IV. ii. 346.)

His divination *is* wrong, however, for the British, with the help of Cymbeline's long-lost boys, win. However, they act, paradoxically, as though they had lost, Cymbeline offering to continue as of old with the payments, and the play ending with a celebration of union. You can feel Shakespeare's sense of Rome's supremacy beside the new strength of Britain; which strength, however, must pay due honour to that Roman greatness which is its prototype. The meaning is clearer if we return to the Soothsayer's vision: he saw the Roman eagle as dissolving into the sunbeams of Britain. When things turn out happily the Soothsayer re-interprets his vision, but, even so, never quite hits the more simple and obvious reading; while we, to-day, can feel Shakespeare's own comment over-arching the thoughts of his dramatic persons.

Here are the final speeches:

Cymbeline :   Well ;
    My peace we will begin. And, Caius Lucius,
    Although the victor, we submit to Caesar,
    And to the Roman empire ; promising
    To pay our wonted tribute, from the which
    We were dissuaded by our wicked queen ;
    Whom heavens—in justice both on her and hers—
    Have laid most heavy hand.
Soothsayer : The fingers of the powers above do tune
    The harmony of this peace. The vision

> Which I made known to Lucius ere the stroke
> Of this yet scarce-cold battle, at this instant
> Is full accomplish'd; for the Roman eagle,
> From south to west on wing soaring aloft,
> Lessen'd herself, and in the beams o' the sun
> So vanish'd : which foreshow'd our princely eagle,
> The imperial Caesar, should again unite
> His favour with the radiant Cymbeline,
> Which shines here in the west.

Cymbeline :   Laud we the gods;
> And let our crooked smokes climb to their nostrils
> From our bless'd altars.   Publish we this peace
> To all our subjects.   Set we forward : let
> A Roman and a British ensign wave
> Friendly together; so through Lud's town march :
> And in the temple of great Jupiter
> Our peace we'll ratify; seal it with feasts.
> Set on there.   Never was a war did cease,
> Ere bloody hands were wash'd, with such a peace.

                                                    (V. v. 459.)

A noble conclusion to this most majestic play, and somewhat
bitter reading at such a period of remorseless warring as ours.
But there is, too, a pagan grandeur, a burning virility, hinted
throughout, which we do well to examine.   The two wild yet
princely boys and their sun-worship, their song about 'golden
lads and girls' (IV. ii. 262), and the eagle dissolving into the
gold blaze of 'radiant Cymbeline', all balance the subtler story of
Posthumus' and Imogen's attainment of marriage integrity, to
build a comprehensive statement of Britain's potential beauty and
power.   Even more clearly than in *Macbeth* and *Lear*, those
historical plays that nevertheless do not appear, on the surface,
to hold precise contemporary meanings, you can feel in *Cymbeline*,
through the often fanciful plot, a sense of England's destiny
pushing through.

In *Henry VIII* Shakespeare ends his life-work with a massive
and closely realistic working out of events within living memory.
This great play is Shakespeare's crowning achievement, though
the understanding of it has been hampered by an utterly un-
founded rumour that some scenes are un-Shakespearian.   To these
objections I have elsewhere (in *The Criterion*, January 1936)
given a full reply.   *Henry VIII* is no mere historical pageant:

it is far nearer a prophetic document, possessing a similarly cul-
minating importance in the last half of Shakespeare's life-work to
that of *Henry V* in the first; and indeed these two plays alone
deliberately solicit the audience's sympathetic co-operation, as
though the task seemed too heavy.   The one prologue echoes the
other.   Compare

> . . . think ye see
> The very persons of our noble story
> As they were living . . .
>
> (Prologue, 25.)

with

> Think, when we talk of horses, that you see them
> Printing their proud hoofs i' the receiving earth.
> (*Henry V*, Chorus—Act I, 26.)

Both plays have contemporary impact: Henry V was in one of
the choruses compared directly to the Earl of Essex.   At first
sight the plan of *Henry VIII* seems unco-ordinated and loose, but
it obeys the same law as Shakespeare's earlier national play, *King
John*; and we must, I fear, again delay our advance to indulge
in short retrospective notice of that play before proceeding further.

In *King John* we have a somewhat untidy story, which can
only be understood as an artistic unit if we feel that the true hero
is England, vaguely, and often unworthily, shadowed by John,
King of England.   That is why Faulconbridge, voice of England's
destiny, assists a king who seems unworthy of so penetrating an
intelligence.   Cardinal Pandulph from Rome is at first an am-
bassador of powerful religious and political authority, inimical to
John and his ways, but the play ends with John's submission and
a consequent union that extends to friendship with France also.
So much is simple.   But there is also severe tragedy in the appalling sufferings caused by John to Constance and her boy, Arthur,
presented with that tragic sympathy of which Shakespeare is the
world's master.   Should we not say, then, that Shakespeare's heart
is in this, and the play's outward form of steady national accomplishment secondary?   We can, if we like.   Nationalism in
Shakespeare is only so supremely important because, in the depths,
he has a sense of the human essence, in joy or pain, that far out-
spaces all national and historic boundaries.   But it is better to

unify our impressions as follows: the process of England's rise to
a national integrity is accompanied by terrible suffering. All the
stock arguments of anti-nationalists and anti-imperialists are thus
potentially present, though sternly controlled, in Shakespeare's
work.

All worldly power is, indeed, sin-struck at the core; and one
cannot finally call any country a merciful power whilst year after
year men and women, who are, in the depths, no more guilty
than their neighbours, are sent to prison and, at the worst, death,
for deeds which they have, certainly, committed, but concerning
which the courts of divine understanding will make a different
ruling from the courts of man. We may remember Portia's
speech in *The Merchant of Venice*, the whole of *Measure for
Measure*, Lear's words in madness on the futility of all justice,
and Timon's curses. All this Shakespeare's genius takes into
account; and, just as in the early *King John* he works through
appalling sufferings of woman and child—and how often in
Shakespeare a woman suffers for or redeems man's turbulent course
—to a final trust in England's destiny, so the whole sequence of
great plays from *Hamlet* to *The Tempest* returns (as, too, did
Shakespeare's whole earlier historic sequence of tragic and bur-
dened kingship and Falstaffian criticism work up to *Henry V*) to
a play explicitly asserting the importance of Great Britain's
historic mission.

Alone among the Histories *Henry VIII* is a play of peace
throughout, the required note being struck in the first scene by
the magnificent description of the Field of the Cloth of Gold.
In the world of Shakespeare's Histories war means either (i) civil
war or (ii) war between England and France. In *Henry V* the
one, and in *Henry VIII* the other, is transcended. For the rest,
the plan of *Henry VIII* resembles that of *King John*, but is more
consciously and symmetrically designed. There are three individual tragedies, all very similar; but the King rises. We watch,
in succession, the falls of Buckingham, Wolsey, and Queen
Katharine. They are all haughty people in the extreme, but, at
their fall, characterised by acceptance and a sense of being, as
Buckingham says of himself, 'half in heaven'. I quote Buckingham's farewell on his way to death, than which there is nothing

nobler in all Shakespeare. Many variations can and should be developed in the acting. This is my reading. Feeling deeply wronged, he shows at first a balance of controlled bitterness and noble resignation; is momentarily disturbed by what may be considered a peculiarly testing request from Lovell, but, mastering himself, rises to a sublime Christian forgiveness; is next stung by another, and this time maddening, interruption, which lances him on the very spot where the accumulated poison of pride yet lingers, so that he gives way to scathing denunciation; and, last, at the second 'all good people', realises suddenly how far he has fallen below that Christlike serenity he had thought to preserve. Here it is:

Buckingham :   All good people,
You that thus far have come to pity me,
Hear what I say, and then go home and lose me.
I have this day received a traitor's judgement,
And by that name must die : yet, heaven bear witness,
And if I have a conscience, let it sink me,
Even as the axe falls, if I be not faithful !
The law I bear no malice for my death ;
'T has done, upon the premises, but justice :
But those that sought it I could wish more Christians :
Be what they will, I heartily forgive 'em.
Yet let 'em look they glory not in mischief,
Nor build their evils on the graves of great men ;
For then my guiltless blood must cry against 'em.
For further life in this world I ne'er hope,
Nor will I sue, although the king have mercies
More than I dare make faults. You few that loved me
And dare be bold to weep for Buckingham,
His noble friends and fellows, whom to leave
Is only bitter to him, only dying,
Go with me, like good angels, to my end,
And, as the long divorce of steel falls on me,
Make of your prayers one sweet sacrifice
And lift my soul to heaven. Lead on, o' God's name.

Lovell : I do beseech your grace, for charity,
If ever any malice in your heart
Were hid against me, now to forgive me frankly.

Buckingham : Sir Thomas Lovell, I as free forgive you
As I would be forgiven : I forgive all.
There cannot be those numberless offences
'Gainst me, that I cannot take peace with : no black envy

Shall mark my grave.　Commend me to his Grace,
And if he speak of Buckingham, pray tell him
You met him half in heaven : my vows and prayers
Yet are the king's, and, till my soul forsake,
Shall cry for blessings on him : may he live
Longer than I have time to tell his years !
Ever beloved and loving may his rule be !
And when old time shall lead him to his end,
Goodness and he fill up one monument !

Lovell :　　To the water side I must conduct your Grace ;
Then give my charge up to Sir Nicholas Vaux,
Who undertakes you to your end.

Vaux :　　　　　　　　　　　　Prepare there ;
The duke is coming : see the barge be ready,
And fit it with such furniture as suits
The greatness of his person.

Buckingham :　　　　　　　　Nay, Sir Nicholas,
Let it alone ; my state now will but mock me.
When I came hither, I was lord high constable
And Duke of Buckingham ; now, poor Edward Bohun :
Yet I am richer than my base accusers,
That never knew what truth meant : I now seal it ;
And with that blood will make 'em one day groan for't.
My noble father, Henry of Buckingham,
Who first raised head against usurping Richard,
Flying for succour to his servant Banister,
Being distress'd, was by that wretch betray'd,
And without trial fell ; God's peace be with him !
Henry the Seventh succeeding, truly pitying
My father's loss, like a most royal prince,
Restored me to my honours, and out of ruins
Made my name once more noble.　Now his son,
Henry the Eighth, life, honour, name and all
That made me happy, at one stroke has taken
For ever from the world.　I had my trial,
And must needs say, a noble one ; which makes me
A little happier than my wretched father.
Yet thus far we are one in fortunes : both
Fell by our servants, by those men we loved most ;
A most unnatural and faithless service !
Heaven has an end in all : yet, you that hear me,
This from a dying man receive as certain :
Where you are liberal of your loves and counsels
Be sure you be not loose ; for those you make friends
And give your hearts to, when they once perceive
The least rub in your fortunes, fall away
Like water from ye, never found again

But where they mean to sink ye.   All good people,
Pray for me !   I must now forsake ye : the last hour
Of my long weary life is come upon me.
Farewell :
And when you would say something that is sad,
Speak how I fell.   I have done ; and God forgive me !

(II. i. 55.)

Never were the unscaleable heights of Christian humility more
subtly defined.   Though he fails of that, see how he regards, like
Henry V, his own faithful retainers as his ' fellows '.   There is
nothing ungenerous or socially exclusive in the Shakespearian
nobility.   What essential grace, what innate aristocracy, these
people express, almost irrespective of all faults and virtues.   They
tread the stage like beings of a higher world than ours.

It is the same with Wolsey.   It was Wolsey who brought
about the disgrace and death of Buckingham, and now he falls in
his turn, and speaks in very nearly the same idiom of religious
assurance.   He realises that ambition has taken him far beyond
his ' depth '.   He is an exemplar of all power-seeking whatsoever,
of man, or party, that does not realise that final power must reside
in that which is beyond man, the crown, or some other such semi-
divine medium; in the highest courts of appeal, that greater
mediator, Christ :

Wolsey :   Cromwell, I did not think to shed a tear
             In all my miseries ; but thou hast forc'd me,
             Out of thy honest truth, to play the woman.
             Let's dry our eyes : and thus far hear me, Cromwell ;
             And, when I am forgotten, as I shall be,
             And sleep in dull cold marble, where no mention
             Of me more must be heard of, say, I taught thee,
             Say, Wolsey, that once trod the ways of glory,
             And sounded all the depths and shoals of honour,
             Found thee a way, out of his wrack, to rise in ;
             A sure and safe one, though thy master miss'd it.
             Mark but my fall, and that that ruin'd me.
             Cromwell, I charge thee, fling away ambition :
             By that sin fell the angels ; how can man then,
             The image of his Maker, hope to win by't ?
             Love thyself last : cherish those hearts that hate thee ;
             Corruption wins not more than honesty.
             Still in thy right hand carry gentle peace,

To silence envious tongues : be just, and fear not.
Let all the ends thou aim'st at be thy country's,
Thy God's, and truth's; then if thou fall'st, O Cromwell !
Thou fall'st a blessed martyr.   Serve the king;
And—prithee, lead me in :
There take an inventory of all I have,
To the last penny; 'tis the king's : my robe,
And my integrity to heaven is all
I dare now call mine own.   O Cromwell, Cromwell !
Had I but serv'd my God with half the zeal
I serv'd my king, he would not in mine age
Have left me naked to mine enemies.

Cromwell :   Good sir, have patience.

Wolsey :   So I have.   Farewell
The hopes of court ! my hopes in heaven do dwell.

                                        (III. ii. 429.)

Without service to God, true service to the King is itself impossible, and so Wolsey must fall.   His faith to both, at the last,
remains: of the King he says 'That sun, I pray, may never set'
(III. ii. 416).   Buckingham, too, asserts at the last his allegiance
to the 'King'; the whole play's theme is, indeed, ' God save the
King '.

Similarly Queen Katharine, cast off, unjustly divorced, and
dying in loneliness, yet blesses the King ' in death '.   She, too,
was proud, and bitter against Wolsey, her wronger.   But a
sublime charity breathes throughout this cathedral of a play.
Griffith, an ordinary gentleman, in soft tones speaks of Wolsey's
better qualities, and the Queen, listening, accepts the charitable
judgment.   She is the last and greatest of Shakespeare's wronged
women, and she, in her dying, enjoys, through that new and
purposive mysticism so urgent in Shakespeare's latest work, a
direct vision of paradise, angels appearing to her in sleep and
wafting her to the joy her earthly pilgrimage has not known.

Now slowly rises the last movement.   Wolsey and the Roman
Church, as with Cardinal Pandulph in *King John*, have bulked
largely in the action.   Continental and Roman Catholic plots
have been something against which the King has had to contend,
getting irritated with Rome and crushing the too ambitious
Wolsey.   But now Cranmer takes the stage, Cranmer who was
destined to be a martyr for the cause of the Reformed Church

in England, and therefore a type of English, as opposed to continental, religious autonomy.   Whereas our three tragic heroes
were excessively proud and fell, each by the King's rejection, so
Cranmer is excessively humble and rises, by the King's grace.
Though the play seems at first merely to record certain known
events, a most subtle treatment is all the time suggesting deeper
and more perennially important significances.   The persons are
all more than themselves: they are instruments, as it were, in the
creation of that England from which Shakespeare's work flowers.

The King, however, is not himself a very impressive man.
Though far from the ' bluff King Hal ' of a later imagination, he
remains somewhat impersonal, certainly not faultless, and seems to
be feeling his way; a strange composite, in which his office as
king is all important while he, as a man, scarcely counts one way
or the other.   As in *King John*, we can feel England's future constitutional monarchy implicit.   Wolsey certainly deserved to fall,
and Buckingham was dangerous.   But the King's divorce of the
childless Katharine is hard to justify, especially since there is no
doubt about the part played by Anne Bullen's attractions.   We
should, however, feel a deeper compulsion working through King
Henry's virtues and vices alike, his considered plans and wayward
desires.   Shakespeare is steadily preparing a synthesis of religious
mysticism with national purpose; and this synthesis is not actually
accomplished in the King himself, but rather in the royal child,
Elizabeth.   The divorce of Katharine is therefore dramatically
justified.   In thus laying the full weight of prophetic emphasis on
a child Shakespeare obeys a fundamental law of the human imagination with analogies in Isaiah, Vergil, and Christianity; for in a
child eternity and time necessarily embrace, and futurity lies
curled.   Therefore we are directed by a choric commentary to
rejoice in the King's rising fortune—for one feels such an advance
—in his new marriage; we applaud his gracious support of the
good Cranmer; and the massive play ends with the christening
ceremony of the baby Elizabeth, over whom Cranmer speaks the
final prophecy, Shakespeare's last word to the England he loved:

> Let me speak, sir,
> For heaven now bids me ; and the words I utter
> Let none think flattery, for they'll find 'em truth.

This royal infant—heaven still move about her!—
Though in her cradle, yet now promises
Upon this land a thousand thousand blessings,
Which time shall bring to ripeness : she shall be—
But few now living can behold that goodness—
A pattern to all princes living with her,
And all that shall succeed : Saba was never
More covetous of wisdom and fair virtue
Than this pure soul shall be : all princely graces,
That mould up such a mighty piece as this is,
With all the virtues that attend the good,
Shall still be doubled on her ; truth shall nurse her ;
Holy and heavenly thoughts still counsel her ;
She shall be lov'd and fear'd ; her own shall bless her ;
Her foes shake like a field of beaten corn,
And hang their heads with sorrow ; good grows with her.
In her days every man shall eat in safety
Under his own vine what he plants ; and sing
The merry songs of peace to all his neighbours.
God shall be truly known ; and those about her
From her shall read the perfect ways of honour,
And by those claim their greatness, not by blood.
Nor shall this peace sleep with her ; but as when
The bird of wonder dies, the maiden phoenix,
Her ashes new-create another heir
As great in admiration as herself,
So shall she leave her blessedness to one—
When heaven shall call her from this cloud of darkness—
Who, from the sacred ashes of her honour,
Shall star-like rise, as great in fame as she was,
And so stand fix'd.   Peace, plenty, love, truth, terror,
That were the servants to this chosen infant,
Shall then be his, and like a vine grow to him :
Wherever the bright sun of heaven shall shine,
His honour and the greatness of his name
Shall be, and make new nations ; he shall flourish,
And, like a mountain cedar, reach his branches
To all the plains about him ; our children's children
Shall see this, and bless heaven.

(V. v. 15.)

As in the early *King John*, we end with a speech of national prophecy, though this has a new depth and quiet assurance born of those great soul-adventures that followed.   Every phrase of it must be weighed, including the reminders of ' fear ' and ' terror '. See how the ' stately cedar ' of *Cymbeline* is transferred to a contemporary monarch, under whom England and Scotland are now unified. Every tragic insight, every penetrating sting of satire, every deepest religious intuition, orthodox or otherwise, of the greater plays, every lyric love of England's natural sweetness, is subdued within this last, almost ritualistic, offering by Shakespeare of himself and his deepest poetic wisdom to Elizabeth and her successor James I, the two sovereigns under whom he lived, wrote his plays, and died. Throughout my essay I have tried to listen to the subtler voice of Shakespeare's poetry, to show how his speeches and persons are all more than they seem to the unresponsive ear; and surely here, if never elsewhere, we can feel that this prophecy is offered not to two temporal rulers alone, but to the essential sovereignty, the golden thread in England's story, that line of kings in *Macbeth* stretching out ' to the crack of doom ', handed down from his day to ours. *Macbeth* was recalled, and Cranmer's lines forecast, by the ' emblems ' used at Anne Bullen's coronation: holy oil, Edward the Confessor's crown, the rod and the ' bird of peace ' (IV. i. 88–9). The conclusion to *Henry VIII* is no mere record of an historic past, but rather the one comprehensive statement in our literature of that peace towards which the world labours and for which Great Britain fights.

VI

THE SOVEREIGN FLOWER

IT is interesting to observe how thinkers, whether as individuals, parties, or nations, are, under the stress of the present conflict, being forced back beyond their recent lines of defence. Pacifism is, unless very deeply held, repudiated, it would seem, in wartime; many have put aside, temporarily, their communism; while the capitalist sees that big business itself depends finally on a national strength no money can buy. One can watch clouds of superficial reasonings being puffed away to reveal facts. But the facing of facts is not, in itself, enough.

In a time of multiplying confusions our record has been, mainly, creditable, if only because we have, not unlike Hamlet, lived through those confusions whilst holding in tension and variously articulating and putting into practice a greater variety of critical thinking than any other of the great powers. But we must now advance, as Shakespeare advanced beyond *Hamlet* and *King Lear*, through *Timon*, to *Henry VIII*.

In this war, we say, we fight in the cause of international justice: but 'justice' will be construed differently by the interested parties in any dispute. 'Law', and, in its normal semi-legal sense, 'right', only exist as such within an ordered community with some central authority; and to render our claims reasonable we must feel, at least in vague outline, the already forming existence of such an order, with Great Britain, if not its central authority, certainly, in view of her historic past and geographical position, its keypoint. The German challenge exceeds any purely national assertion and is far closer to world-revolution, attacking the root-principles of that growing imperial and international structure, or organism, which Britain consciously or unconsciously fosters. Therefore, when the rumble of a risen Germany grew more menacing, it inevitably fell to Great Britain, as a nation, and not to communism, democracy, or the Christian Church, to oppose it. Russia and the United States, quite naturally, thought first of themselves; while the main emphasis

of established religion, Catholic or Protestant, remains trans-
cendental, with, as things are, slight political influence.

Great Britain, too, was thinking of herself, and did her best to
circumnavigate the vortex; but nevertheless *she cannot, however
much she wishes it, think of herself without thinking of the whole
world*. She, or providence, has worked herself into a position
from which there is no escape. She must, and it is an extremely
awkward destiny, either fall or lead; must, much as she may
scorn, hate, or—and perhaps this is the deeper truth—fear the
thought, reaffirm her power and purpose across the world.

This will be to continue, more self-consciously, what has
already led to her imperial greatness; to increase rather than
decrease it, aiming, and it is not easy, to expand, without dissi-
pating, her strength. A recent leading article in *The Times* drew
a valuable distinction between ' imperialism ' and ' domination ',
seeing both the Roman and the British empires as characterised by
a will to inclusion, not only of peoples, but of their peculiar indi-
vidualities and ways of thought; while also suggesting that such
imperial control was properly a temporary, but of course very
long range, expedient, willing finally its own loss, or self-realisation,
in a yet greater totality.

It is, surely, foolish to expect any such total order to come
about by a planned co-operation of supposedly reasonable entities.
Great things are never so created, nor are human entities, particularly as groups, reasonable. Nor will unity be created by
the iron force of Germanic domination. No. Organic existence
can only mature from what already has organic life. It is far too
usual an error to start planning from above, from the rationalising
centres, whilst neglecting some already living attempt that stands
in need of encouragement and nurture. What is to survive must
grow naturally, like poetry, which, says Keats, if it does not come
as naturally as the leaves to a tree, those branching cedars of
Cymbeline and *Henry VIII*, had better not come at all:

> Our poesy is as a gum which oozes
> From whence 'tis nourish'd. The fire i' the flint
> Shows not till it be struck; our gentle flame
> Provokes itself, and like the current flies
> Each bound it chafes.
> (*Timon of Athens*, I. i. 21.)

So the poet in *Timon* distinguishes the mechanical and fiery from the more instinctive process. Now Keats' words are, I think, quite as true of empire as of poetry, and probably no empire has grown more spontaneously than the British. Trade, the primary medium of England's expansion, is certainly rooted in the soil of personal initiative as mass military aggression can never be. Nevertheless to Keats poetry is also ' might half slumbering on its own right arm ' and, since it relies on inexhaustible sources of energy beyond rational understanding and control, the ' supreme of power '. Likewise the organic growth of our empire has been accompanied by, whilst never exactly subservient to, the exercise of strong action; such strength being one constituent, not the aim, of the creative purpose; which purpose is, in its own way, itself a supreme power, there being no greater or more masterly powers than those of Shakespeare's ' great creating nature '.

We must therefore expect and work for a more self-conscious extension and expansion of Britain's already formed imperial growth, yet not planning from any rigid imperialistic design, but rather getting back at all costs to that central core from which her imperial strength has hitherto branched, and re-nurturing that. Therefore it is that I urge the incomparable necessity of re-awakening the national imagination, which means a renewed respect for our poetic, and particularly our Shakespearian, heritage; since in a vital understanding of Shakespeare's work lie the seed and germ of a greater Britain. Shakespeare speaks, moreover, to nations beyond the Empire, especially to the United States of America, related to us by the greatest of all bonds, the bond of language and therefore of great poetry; and also, since his work has already ' set a girdle round about the world ' to encompass, in spite of linguistic barriers, the whole of civilisation, it may be felt now as a rainbow arch above the flooding fields of war promising, in the lovely phrase of the Sonnets, ' olives of endless age ' to mankind.

In order to serve such a world-wide purpose, our own social and political system must be newly understood and purged of all rottenness, regaining direct contact with sources of strength. Why has the National-Socialist movement in Germany had so strong a hold over its youth? Have we nothing to learn from it? I think we have, but only in order to repenetrate, re-express, and fulfil our own national destiny, which is, potentially, one certainly no less great, and probably far more inclusive, than that of Germany. There must be many changes bearing heavily on the shallow purposes of big business and the equally shallow criticism which it has spawned on all sides. But no party, as such, must be allowed exclusive rights in our thinking. As in Shakespeare warrior idealisation and its obverse of ironic criticism, revolutionary fervour and governmental authority, justice and mercy, worldly ambition and religious humility, masculine strength and feminine love, are all balanced, harmonised, and integrated, so our British constitution has room for capitalist initiative as well as socialist reform, for armed strength as well as pacifist counsel; but our sole final allegiance is to that whole of which all these are parts and whose symbol is the Crown.

Capitalism has a bad name to-day, and much of the mud flung at it is deserved. But not all. In two Shakespearian plays, *The Merchant of Venice* and *Timon of Athens*, riches are a primary theme, and in both they are contrasted with a greater value. In the one we have three caskets, of gold, silver and lead, with the prize of love housed within the meaner metal to drive home the deceptiveness of a superficial brilliance; and, later, laws made for money-transactions are very subtly shown to be unsuitable, indeed illogical, where the supreme good of life itself is at stake.* In *Timon of Athens* all worldly riches are felt as either insubstantial or definitely evil once they cease to serve a sacramental purpose as the outward sign and symbol of an inward communion between man and man. But, and the 'but' is most important, the gold-essence is never repudiated. Portia, figure of grace and love, is herself rich; and the once princely and generous Timon, at his story's end, digs gold from his wild retreat, and is still sought after, remaining in savage nakedness a spiritual aristocrat if ever there was one, concentrating yet on his gold however he may

---

* The economic implications of the trial scene were first pointed out by Max Plowman in ' Money and the Merchant ', the *Adelphi Magazine*, Sept. 1931; and (independently) by Lt.-Col. A. Hanbury-Sparrow in *Gilt-Edged Insecurity*, 1933. See also my *Principles of Shakespearian Production*; and Mr. C. S. Lewis' *Hamlet, the Prince or the Poem.*

G

curse it, obeying his old compulsion to give, and handing it to all who come with imprecations that turn, like those of the Hebrew prophet, to blessings as we read them; while even reforming a bandit by urging him to wholesale destruction and theft. Timon treasures the richer values in himself: they are, to Shakespeare, themselves indestructible however widely they may be falsified. Therefore the gold of human virtue, of love, of life itself, must be safeguarded, and the essence of capitalism, which is merely individual responsibility, freedom, enterprise, and power, is not necessarily at fault. It needs only subjection to that other gold of the community's life, the Crown, wherein not only the general good but also that sum of the human personality, on whose rights capitalism bases its own structure, is richly maintained.

It is the same with socialism. The bubble of communist revolution under a proletariat dictator Shakespeare pricked finally (as far as he was concerned) in the comedy of Jack Cade's rebellion in *2 Henry VI*, with comic reflections in the citizen riot in *Julius Caesar* and Gonzalo's Utopian dreams in *The Tempest*. But when the socialist advances, as I have before suggested that he should, his indictment in terms splendid as those of John of Gaunt's denunciation in *Richard II*, he will be newly empowered, while to let any ' dictatorship of the proletariat ', to borrow a communist phrase, usurp the throne of sovereignty is to insult intelligence and alienate sympathy. Lord Byron's two greatest plays, *Marino Faliero* and *Sardanapalus*, are very pertinent to the advancing social consciousness of Europe. Unwilling to sever contact with traditional allegiances, and possessing a truly Shakespearian feeling for sovereignty, as such, the poet dramatises tales of (i) a revolutionary ' doge ', or duke, that is, very nearly, king, of medieval Venice, who is infuriated by a decadent nobility; and (ii) a socialist and pacifically inclined king of Assyria in the ancient world, who is likewise sickened by a meaningless waste of military bloodshed and a crude imperialism. Both rulers have their faults, and one must not draw any simple conclusions and father them on the poet; but most urgent contemporary issues are in these plays compressed, with a dramatic vigour of high importance relying on a fusion of qualities usually opposed. Byron himself, the revolutionary aristocrat, may be taken as symbolic of the more nobly conceived socialism that we need, a socialism speaking in terms not merely of remedial legislation covering the bodily welfare of a certain class, but crying out against the wrongs done against not only the body but the soul of the nation as a whole by class selfishness and suicidal incompetence. The Crown is as much a possession of the poorest as of the richest; indeed, it should itself function like the sun, soaking up and next redistributing, as a heart, the fluidities of wealth, whilst radiating also warmth and divine joy throughout the nation; and therefore those who have just complaints and a vital social message may claim its fullest sanction. But if they will not, or cannot, do this, or regard such allegiance as either puerile or shameful, we shall suspect them to be half-consciously aware that their message does not pierce beyond a transient and brittle welfare, and even fear lest their socialism serves a destructive, rather than a creative, end.

As for that much-bandied and much-abused word ' democracy ', what of it ? No one, I suppose, really desires a pure democracy, government by the people alone being scarcely desirable and certainly impossible; at least, ' the people ' must be taken to include those long dead and those not yet born to render such a system worthy, for the present is directly answerable to both. Many honourable traditions and a subtle sense also of future direction must play their part in any government which is not to be wholly ephemeral and undisciplined. The people can, as Shakespeare suggests in *Julius Caesar*, be easily manipulated by a mastermind, and in our day of mass propaganda the dangers are great. Except in *Julius Caesar* Shakespeare's greater persons are not involved in any fight for freedom: being kings or nobles they already have it, and the dramatist is concerned rather with their use of it. Freedom is never an end in itself: or rather true freedom, as opposed to licence, is not easily come by without some degree of discipline and education. A perfect democracy must refuse to educate its children; for education presupposes certain more or less unchanging values and principles and an aristocracy—as well in Soviet Russia as democratic Britain—to give them life and expression. Such an aristocracy need not remain one of blood-descent, nor should it, I think, be either intellectual or capitalist. Both in Henry V's ' Crispin ' speech and Cranmer's prophecy at the conclusion of *Henry VIII*, the aristocratic essence is to be distinguished from birth and related to 'honour', to which we may add the 'cunning' (i.e. wisdom) and 'virtue' of Cerimon in *Pericles*, words in which power is, I think, suggested. Self-deception and a thousand dangers wait round the corner, I know; and a democratic liberalism must necessarily function as a vital constituent, as one main aid toward realisation of that greater and exceedingly complex whole of past, present, and future, historic tradition and prophetic destiny, of which the Crown itself, and nothing else, is symbol.

If Great Britain has uniquely succeeded in preserving her royalistic tradition whilst incorporating also a high degree of democratic freedom, that is because her people can on the whole be trusted not to falsify their heritage. There is accordingly tension without internal conflict, and a deep-seated if unformulated faith that all must be well 'if England to herself do rest but true'; if, that is, she remains true to the Shakespearian world, where any one person—as opposed to crowds—is, however low his social status, given by the artist something of a royal integrity. There remains the danger that she will not preserve this truth:

> That England, that was wont to conquer others
> Hath made a shameful conquest of itself.

Hero after hero in Shakespeare works through inward conflict to self-recognition: Katharine the Shrew, Benedick and Beatrice, Richard II, all the great tragic heroes, Cleopatra who is noble to 'herself' in her dying, Leontes, Wolsey with his 'I know myself now'—all follow the one pattern toward self-realisation. Shakespeare's broader thinking sees nations, and in particular England, as suffering, like single persons, from self-deception and self-conflict, even the comedies working generally across a background of civil disunity. But there is always the greater compulsion, as when in *King John* the revolted Salisbury returns to loyalty:

> We will untread the steps of damned flight,
> And like a bated and retired flood,
> Leaving our rankness and irregular course,
> Stoop low within those bounds we have o'erlook'd,
> And calmly run on in obedience
> Even to our ocean, to our great King John.
>
> (V. iv. 52.)

The barons of Shakespeare's historical plays are the various parties of to-day, but the same truth holds, now as then. Liberty is not licence; man obeys a destiny greater than his own understanding; and that destiny is discovered, not by Macbeth's occultist agonies, but by a loyalty which is self-discovery and self-realisation. Shakespeare ultimately has a greater trust in man as man than many a more obviously daring interpreter; and likewise Great Britain, in trusting her own people with wide political rights and expecting other nations to do the same, shows a faith in human nature, in the basic goodness of human instinct, which the Germanic ideal of forceful domination with a view to further violent action contradicts. Shakespeare trusts in an ultimate unity and believes, like Wordsworth in his great ode on immortality, on the royal destinies of mankind.

The balance of man and office in *Richard II, King John*, and *Henry VIII* reflects at once an acknowledgment of discrepancy and a foresight, the story of Richard II actually prefiguring that of Charles I and the process of political development in which his life and death are crucial. Shakespeare's plays, historical or otherwise, owe their tough persistence and ever-yielding richness to a realisation of personal and communal complexities as forcibly projected into imagery and symbol as into the plot-story and its hero-king; and his steady reservations, whether humorous or tragic, concerning power-values are very precisely reflected in our constitution.

The present function of the Crown is a super-rational function, with a reliance on the imagination where logical reasoning fails and a trust in paradox akin to that of Christian symbolism. The conception touches both humour and tragic insight. The nation's ruler is utterly dependent on his ministers' advice, at once semi-divine in office and yet less powerful than his lowest subject on election-days, being, indeed, the one man in the nation without political power. Shakespeare's Hal and Byron's Sardanapalus, both conceived as attractive, indeed ideal, though unconventional, sovereign types who embarrass their respective societies (and bear, I think, an important relation to our own Edward VIII), are humorous types also. These are men who as living individuals embody, rather than symbolise, the semi-mystic properties of kingship, and are therefore the less obviously suitable for their constitutional position, and will be either super-kings or failures, or both at once. The baffling paradox of the Crown witnesses, as do all great humour and great tragedy alike, a salutary recognition of ultimate failure, of ultimate human impossibilities; while, in its turn, conditioning a host of positives. A personal centre is needed to safeguard the sanctity of personality, dramatise the greater self of each subject, and deliver the nation from the paralysis of the abstract concept. The Crown preserves the more magical radiations of the hero-leader without the attendant risks; for the one final essential of a personal centre is that he should not remain, as a person, final.

The design of a Shakespearian play is—and in this Shakespeare follows Lyly—closely related to the queen-centred society of Tudor England. But the king himself, and there is nearly always a king or duke, is not necessarily the hero; nor is the hero himself always, or indeed often, the play's true centre. The king or hero tries to identify himself with something that almost necessarily eludes personification and may be felt as hinted rather by the poetic imagery and certain outstanding symbolisms, such as the magic handkerchief in *Othello*, the weirdly-wild tempest in *King Lear*, the crowned and tree-bearing child in *Macbeth*, or the mysterious music in *Antony and Cleopatra*. Now these, which utter deep, non-rational truths obscure to the persons themselves, correspond more directly to the Crown in our system. They focus the whole drama; just as Richard II when added to his necessary failure, but not Richard alone, points towards a constitutional monarchy. Such symbols bind and redistribute the action, fuse and direct disparate energies, opening vistas of the eternal which the thinking hero does not see. Similarly the Crown to-day is the heart of the nation's body as the prime-minister, or parliament, its rationalising head; drawing to it and redistributing the life-fluid, as London is the heart of our country's economic life with roads and railways as arteries. The heart beats and functions silently, but it is always there and always awake, as the mind is not, conditioning the activities of limb, of eye, and of thought, imitating those sovereign powers of nature which, says Pope in writing of poetry, ' work without show and, without pomp, preside'; a phrase recalling the 'mild majesty and sobre pomp' of Burke's characterisation of the British state in his essay on the French Revolution. Certainly the greatest creative work is accomplished when the mind is sunk within the whole act being performed; a nation may be slowly fulfilling a destiny which its best leaders themselves do not always understand; and many an action of minister or party raising sharpest criticism may also be felt as working within, and as part of, a whole not to be subjected to a facile judgment.

Of this whole the Crown is itself a symbol, and, being in essence an holistic conception, serves as the one bond of unity in an empire otherwise mainly composed of autonomous states. The Crown is, then, both heart and whole of the nation, or empire; and therefore reflects at once its historic heritage, present soul-poten-tiality, and future destiny. To-day many a thinker urges that man's religious consciousness must necessarily be confined to the social organism, while others put sole trust in the established church; but what is best in both tendencies will be subsumed under a vital royalism, pointing towards both a new social order and a newly empowered and authoritative Christianity. The Crown is a dynamic and inexhaustible symbol piercing into realms of the infinite and eternal; it shadows more even than a 'destiny', touching that higher otherness and its purposes *for which the nation exists on earth*; and 'God save the King' asks something even vaster and deeper than national preservation.

Shakespeare does not stand alone: he is father to a line of poets who in the mass balance that one massive life-work. They in turn accentuate this or that side of it, but he only, unless perhaps we may set beside him Lord Byron, is comprehensive. My ex-position of Byron's work appears in *The Burning Oracle*, and I can here do no justice to it, nor to the many other writers deserving our attention. Two important emphases drive through our litera-ture: nature, and especially English nature, as in Pope's *Windsor Forest*, Wordsworth's *Tintern Abbey* and *The Prelude*, and Hardy's Wessex; and the sea, so powerful in Byron, Wordsworth, and Tennyson. All this is deeply Shakespearian. The Histories are rich, however violent the argument or action, in reminders of that English countryside such turbulences deface. Shakespeare's

more gentle, lyric, and pastoral understanding roots from the Warwickshire of his birth, taking poetic form in woodland fairies and
forest glades; and I wonder what the subdued yet rich and fertile
luxuriance of ' England's green and pleasant land ', together with
its rich variety, has had to do with her widespread and enduringly
creative work throughout the last three centuries, expanding from
this tiny island to make, as Shakespeare's Cranmer says, ' new
nations '.   I am reminded of an exquisite miniature in *Macbeth*
condensing wide areas of the Shakespearian gospel.   As they press
towards victory, the saving forces swear they will pour out, if
needed for their ' country's purge ', each drop of themselves

> To dew the sovereign flower and drown the weeds.
>
> (V. ii. 30.)

That is, to plant young Malcolm on Scotland's throne. ' Sovereign flower ': a magical excellence is hinted, as in ' sovereign
remedy ', yet nature is preserved.   Indeed, Shakespeare's nature-
feeling is one in kind with his royalistic doctrine; hence his continual equation of kingship with the sun, and both those, variously,
with human love—as in *The Merchant of Venice*, *Troilus and
Cressida*, and the Sonnets—preserving throughout the royalty of
the romantic imagination.

As for the sea, it thunders in passage after Shakespearian passage,
and is indeed Shakespeare's main poetic symbol, its roughness
especially being used over and over again to impress on us a sense
of man's turbulent existence, with a storm-tossed boat as a recurrent symbol forman's buffeted soul.   Naturally enough his last
play but one, planned to capture the essence of his total poetry, is
called *The Tempest*.   Now Britain's power has been pre-eminently
a sea-power and her political story one of a semi-nautical skill, a
veering to the winds, her immediate goal often unknown, but
trusting, with a navigator's instinct, to the stars.   Germany's
assertion is a land-assertion, upstanding and jagged, like a mountain rock, and thickly clustered with armed might as the massive
tree-legions of the Black Forest.   I feel a relation between the
sea and the vaster powers; and in the present war it seems proper
enough that England should be outnumbered on land, and yet, if
a wider space and longer period be taken, should expect to gain,

in her turn, from a strength due to imperial expansion and sea-mastery.

On our coins we have pictured Britannia, with shield and helmet and a trident to signify control of the sea.   She resembles Pallas Athene, goddess of wisdom, and on our latest pound notes we have two such persons, one bearing an olive branch, for peace, and another, as a water-mark, helmeted and with a Greek profile. The sea is the great realm of subconscious, pre-animal, life, and its mastery may be equated with mastery of instinct and therefore highest wisdom.   Great Britain has been for long at pains to train and humanise the savage and bestial instincts, spurning their attack :

> England bound in by the triumphant sea
> Whose rocky shore beats back the envious siege
> Of watery Neptune . . .

Browning talks of the ' snaky sea ', and the association of sea and reptile life is normal enough; and I once, in *Atlantic Crossing*, suggested that Nelson was set towering over all London's heroes because he was ' master of the great dragon ', and a ' reincarnated Saint George '.   Our pound notes picture not only Britannia, but also Saint George slaying the Dragon.

A rough sea in Shakespeare's poetry is over and over again associated with wild beasts, and we have noticed the regularity with which dangerous instincts are said to make man bestial, as in *The Merchant of Venice*, where Gratiano suggests that a wolf's soul has found its way into the human form of Shylock.   Bears, wolves, and boars I have elsewhere termed Shakespeare's ' tempest-beasts ' ; Coriolanus is compared to a dragon—so is Lear in his first wrath—and Richard III called a ' cacodemon '; and so on. Last comes Caliban, the fish-monster, at once beast, savage, and semi-devil.

Against Caliban is Ariel, air and fire as against earth and water, angelic and swift; and so against Shakespeare's tempest-beasts are his hounds, especially greyhounds, and horses.   These are swift and graceful; and we may remember both the musical hounds on which Theseus, the perfection of knighthood, rhapsodises in *A Midsummer Night's Dream*, and the fine horses of good King Duncan, ' beauteous and swift, the minions of their race ', in

Macbeth (II. iv. 15).   Both hounds and horses are highly honoured
in *Henry V*, and in Shakespeare's first poem, *Venus and Adonis*,
we have two animals, good and bad: Adonis' finely described
horse and the ugly, murderous, boar.   It is a hunting poem, and
hounds are sympathetically described; hunting often in literature
serving to suggest virility without inhumanity, as in the imagery
of *Henry V*, and with Theseus and Timon, the 'princely boys' in
Cymbeline, and Coleridge's remarkable play *Zapolya*.   Such poetry
aspires to the symbolism of Saint George.

Shakespeare has, too, images of angelic grace athletically per-
ceived, as when Hamlet sees his father's poise as

> A station like the herald Mercury
> New lighted on a heaven-kissing hill,
>
> (III. iv. 58.)

or Romeo sees his love as a 'winged messenger of Heaven'
bestriding the clouds (II. ii. 28); or Macbeth imagines 'Heaven's
cherubin horsed upon the sightless couriers of the air' (I. vii. 22).
These are riding figures, and athletic; and so, in characterising
man's semi-divine nature, Hamlet says of him 'in action how
like an angel', but 'in apprehension, how like a god' (II. ii.
325–6).   One is not surprised that Prince Hal in *Henry IV* should
be described in terms of a mercurial horsemanship:

> I saw young Harry with his beaver on,
> His cuisses on his thighs, gallantly arm'd,
> Rise from the ground like feather'd Mercury,
> And vaulted with such ease into his seat,
> As if an angel dropp'd down from the clouds,
> To turn and wind a fiery Pegasus
> And witch the world with noble horsemanship.
>
> (*1 Henry IV*, IV. i. 104.)

Pegasus was the mythical flying horse on which Bellerophon, a
dragon-slayer like Perseus and Saint George (himself a reincarna-
tion of Saint Michael), was mounted.   'Young Harry' is Shakespeare's picturisation of ideal English youth; and Shakespeare's
athletic and mercurial imagery certainly fits that aerial skill and
heroism of our own day likely to prove as important henceforth
in our national story as sea-adventure in the past.   This speech is

throughout light, volatile, aerial, with bird-references and cleverly used i-vowels in the lines preceding my quotation—'estridges', 'eagles', 'glittering', 'spirit'—as well as thoughts of bathing and comparison with 'May' and young animals. But against it the more Germanic Hotspur next speaks, with rounded o-sounds, anxious to offer his opponents 'all hot and bleeding' to the 'fire-eye'd maid of smoky war', visualising the 'mailéd Mars' sitting 'up to the ears in blood'. Hotspur's 'horse' is to bear him like a 'thunderbolt' against 'the bosom of the Prince of Wales'. He ends with a fine couplet:

> Harry to Harry shall, hot horse to horse,
> Meet and ne'er part till one drop down a corse.
>
> (IV. i. 122.)

Heavy, thudding, impactuous sounds and cruel imagery are balanced against aerial brilliance and an almost sportive military excellence.

The more violent energies are, however, to be respected, and on occasion the lion or tiger is used to figure a noble ferocity, but the Saint George symbol, if not too precisely urged, holds good: even when he writes a pure farce, Shakespeare calls it *The Taming of the Shrew*. Similarly Great Britain's story has been one of a steady humanising, both in her traditional, somewhat puritanical, ethic at home and her civilising mission abroad, playing Prospero to beast Caliban. So on our pound notes, as once on our golden sovereigns, we have Saint George on his prancing charger with Roman helmet and sword, slaying his dragon. He is, like so much in Shakespeare, a compound of the Roman and the Christian, and his job the quelling of those dragon-forces that so easily disrupt human existence. He is chivalric: that is, he symbolises strength without brutality, which is, indeed, suggested by the name Shake-speare itself. A quatrain from Dryden's opera *King Arthur* describes him:

> Saint George, the Patron of our Isle,
> A soldier and a saint,
> On that auspicious order smile,
> Which love and arms will plant.

He figures, too, as 'guardian' of our land, in one of Wordsworth's odes written in celebration of an English victory; while to-day he appears in G. K. Chesterton's

> I am Saint George, whose cross in scutcheon scored
> Red as the Rose of England on me glows.
> The Dragon who would pluck it found this sword
> Which is the thorn upon the English Rose.

Shakespeare's reputed birthday is 23rd April, Saint George's Day; which seems natural enough, and if it be by design the more significant for that.

What do these symbols mean to us? To draw attention to them at this hour will seem, perhaps, a trifle silly to many of my readers. Yet they are on every note we spend, stamped on the golden currency of our social life, the elixirs of private wealth. I am urging no new discoveries or new readings. I can truly say with Antony, 'I tell you that which you yourselves do know'. I merely interpret for us our own national myth, and my remarks are in the main highway and central tradition of our literature. Poetry is the only true wisdom, and it is not widely enough recognised how it affects, or should affect, as our philosophical theologies and political theorisings do not, the seats of action.

But, you may say, neither the works of Shakespeare, nor our Britannia and Saint George symbolisms, no, nor the Crown, need necessarily possess those meanings I attribute to them, nor exert those compulsions I urge. No—they need not. Poetic perception, like religious faith, is no passive acquiescence, but rather an active co-operation, the very truth concerned being dynamic and needing, as does the actor's art, a lively response for its realisation. While we remain sluggish in our reception of literature and the national myth we fail necessarily to respond to the Crown itself, which is an essentially poetic, indeed dramatic, conception, a make-believe utterly dependent—and therein lies its supreme value—on our creative participation: it is more than a safeguard of our freedom; it is a means of forcing it. Why do we append 'God Save the King' to our musical and dramatic and cinema performances? Surely because all such ritual—for ritual it is, however popular the entertainment offered—is an approach to the high drama of the Crown. Our national life does not rise above the dramatic, but aspires to it; and the faculty of the dramatic imagination is not, as so often supposed, secondary, but sovereign. To-day we have slight national imagination, except in times of peril, which is like having no religion except when ill; and where there is no imagination, the people, sooner or later, perish.

Therefore I reassert the necessity of understanding afresh our national symbolisms in crown, in patron emblems, and in literature. All these we must know as dynamic, not merely historic; must feel them not only as they are, but as they might be to an awakened comprehension. The great poetry of our past is a treasure-casket laid by for the hour of need, charged accumulators awaiting contact. Maybe we cannot feel glamorously, as does Germany, about our own destiny. We have risen beyond cheap and destruc-tive nationalisms; but we must now rise further to a new national faith, nobler than any yet known on earth. We cannot go back. We must press on, and up. We can, moreover, do what Germany cannot, search within our own literature for authoritative inspira-tion and re-infection with that virus we so sorely need. True, Shakespeare is probably more widely loved in Germany than in England; and I confess that certain Shakespearian depths of the metaphysical imagination are more sensitively received in Germany than by us. But such a response is surely potential in us too, for we, not Germany, produced Shakespeare, just as we, not Germany, invented aeroplanes, and even tanks. Shakespeare's total impact is, moreover, apart from any explicit nationalism, superbly British: with its greater comprehensiveness and balanc-ing of opposites, its respect to the softer values, and use of those two integrating factors so important as unifiers of instinctive energy and the rationalising consciousness, the sense of sin and the sense of humour, both of which the Germanic temperament lacks.

To-day two ways of life are opposed. As in Shakespearian tragedy the psychic conflict of the middle action expresses itself in outward military opposition towards the end, so, reversing the process, we can see, beneath our present armed contest, an ancient, if somewhat rusty, pseudo-Christian culture challenged by keen forces that have steadily gathered in Europe since the Renaissance. This is no mere question of national boundaries or possessions: rather the powers grouped against each other, as 'mighty opposites' of causes stretching beyond themselves and their own time, wrestle for the mastery of man's soul.   Our joint destiny must, I think, involve a fusion of the very powers now seemingly engaged in death-grapple: 'the red rose and the white are on his face . . .' The Dragon—as Nietzsche knew—has his rights.   The demonic energies that Shakespeare's art so beautifully controls are yet the raw stuff of his greatest poetry, his music.   Each play is a ritual whereby internal discord is objectified in war, and war transmuted into peace; until the whole succession culminates in that vision of British peace outlined by Cranmer's prophecy in *Henry VIII*.   So the two principles of unity in Shakespeare—his tempests and his nationalism—converge; and since his day Great Britain has worked, in the wider context, to make harmony of discords.   This task Englishmen must henceforth continue with a will to the service, not of a nation, nor even an empire, but a world.   This will be the task of a Great Britain which, if it does not claim to be, as a nation, or empire, purely Christian, is yet a nation long chosen and self-dedicated to creative labour across the globe, and which, through a sovereign henceforth not only defender but also advancer of the Faith, may approach, without shame, the throne of Christ.